Staff Development
in Academic Libraries

Present practice and future challenges

Edited by
Margaret Oldroyd

Staff Development Manager, Division of Learning Development,
De Montfort University

Library Association Publishing
London

Published by
Library Association Publishing
7 Ridgmount Street
London WC1E 7AE

First published 1996

British Library Cataloguing in Publication Data
A catalogue record for this book is available from the British Library

ISBN 1-85604-174-3

Typeset from authors' disks in 11/13pt Palermo and Arial by Library Association Publishing
Printed and made in Great Britain by Bookcraft (Bath) Ltd

Contents

List of Contributors

Robert Bluck is Faculty Services Manager at the University of Northumbria Information Services. He was a teacher and Open University tutor before becoming a librarian, and has worked as a subject librarian and site librarian in academic libraries.

Professor Mel Collier is responsible for libraries, computing, networking, media services, teaching and learning development and staff development at De Montfort University. His current interests include the management of teaching and learning in the expanding university sector with particular reference to electronic library concepts and multimedia. He writes and speaks regularly on these and other aspects of management of change. He is chair of the British Council Libraries and Information Advisory Committee, chair of the Management Committee of the UK Office for Library Networking (UKOLN) and serves on the Ministerial Advisory Committee for the European Libraries Plan (ACELP). He leads a major programme in electronic library research and was rapporteur recently in the finalization of the Fourth Framework Telematics Programme for Libraries in Brussels.

Susan Jurow is the Director of the Association of Research Libraries' Office in Management Services. She monitors emerging professional and managerial issues in order to provide leadership for the Association's management training, consulting, management information, and diversity programs.

Maxine Melling is Principal Librarian at the University of Central Lancashire, where her responsibilities include the management and planning of staff training and of the Library's quality initiatives. Her background is in a range of academic libraries, in both further and higher education.

Patrick Noon has worked in academic libraries for almost 25 years and is currently University Librarian at Coventry University. He is a member of SCONUL's Advisory Committee on Staffing and of The Library Association's Personnel Training and Education Group.

Robert Oldroyd is Deputy Librarian at the University of Nottingham. He has management responsibility for Human Resources, including training and staff development, appraisal and job evaluation. He was a founder member of the Information and Library Services Lead Body, developing S/NVQs for our employment sector.

Margaret Oldroyd is a chartered librarian with 20 years experience of library management in further and higher education. She is Staff Development Manager in the Division of Learning Development at De Montfort University with responsibility for human resource management in this converged service. She also manages the University's staff development programme for teaching staff.

Julie Parry is Dean of Libraries and Learning Support at Bath College of Higher Education. She has run CPD workshops and training events over a number of years. Her publications include articles and training guides on various aspects of managing people in library and information services.

Professor Patricia Partington is Executive Director of the UK Universities' and Colleges' Staff Development Agency, established by The Committee of Vice-Chancellors and Principals of the Universities of the United Kingdom. The Agency has remit to support and advise UK universities on training and development for all categories of staff. Patricia previously worked as a researcher and Lecturer in Education at the Universities of Nottingham and Sheffield. Between 1985 and 1989 she established a human resources development unit at the University of Sheffield. She has wide experience of the planning and delivery of continuing professional development for all staff in higher education.

Nik Pollard is Head of Computing and Library Services at Kingston University. He has a particular interest in the role of libraries in new learning meethods, especially resource-based learning. He is one of the authors of *Institutional Support for Resource Based Learning* published by the Oxford Centre for Staff Development.

Phil Sykes is Learning Resources Manager at Liverpool John Moores University's innovative 'ARC', where he manages an integrated library and computing service. His principal professional interests are staff development, staff management and motivation, and the opportunities and challenges offered by 'convergence'.

Introduction

MARGARET OLDROYD

> Failure to provide library staff with adequate training and to deploy them effectively represents one of the single most important constraints on change and development in library and information provision, and can seriously undermine its effectiveness, especially when this depends on the implementation of new practices, or on information technology.[1]

This statement is one with which it is hard to disagree, particularly when the only constant factor in academic libraries, and their parent institutions, seems to be change! In comparison, it is very easy to argue about why the failure occurs – is it lack of money or time, poor understanding of the role of training, inadequate strategic and operational planning? Staff development in relation to change management at organizational, library and individual levels is a key issue in this book.

The Fielden Report[2] recommends that institutions 'should consciously plan' for the people who will be responsible for putting their library and information service plans into effect, with particular reference to changing staff roles. It is the management of staff development and training, in the context of human resource management and in relation to institutional and library planning, which is the focus of this book. Its central concern is not the techniques of training delivery, but rather the current context and issues and future challenges for this area of strategic management.

Some of the issues which have influenced universities and colleges in the last decade can be summarized as

- growth in student numbers without a parallel rise in resources
- changes in teaching and learning methods
- increasingly diverse student population
- continuous rapid change

- the need to manage resources on a value-for-money basis
- the requirement for customer-centred, high quality services
- developments in information technology.

Institutions are required by the Funding Councils to respond to these, and many other issues, by creating strategic plans which define their mission, aims and objectives. The efficient and effective use of human resources is a key element in the implementation of those plans. The requirement to operate with maximum efficiency has led to a reduction in staff, reviews of the relative roles of different groups of staff and changing library staffing structures. Most recently, the first initiatives resulting from the Follett Report[1] have produced a rash of new library buildings and IT development projects, themselves creating new challenges for the management and development of staff.

It is the contention of the Fielden Report[3] that effective staff development, which meets the needs of the new environment, will best result from systematic management of the function. Each library must have a staff development policy. Needs should be analysed, plans drawn up, resources allocated, and the implementation of the resulting programmes evaluated in order to inform the next training cycle. All this is to be the responsibility of a senior library manager. The chapter on the national staff development framework, together with those which examine the concept of continuing professional development and the role of appraisal and personal development planning systems, address key aspects of such a framework.

Subsequent chapters analyse the impact on staff development of various quality systems and initiatives, changing roles of staff in resource-based and student-centred learning, and the proliferation of converged learning support services in relation to present practice and future needs. Further chapters consider the evolving roles of the three major groups of library staff highlighted in the Fielden Report – library assistants, subject librarians, heads of service – and comment on development issues and the needs of each in the context previously outlined.

But even if the staff development and training function of academic libraries is systematically managed, is it fully integrated with other processes to produce a strategic approach to human resource management?

During the last 10 years there has been a changed approach to staff development and training, which is part of a more general shift from the concept of personnel management to that of human resource management. Personnel management is seen as a reactive approach, emphasizing industrial relations and the welfare problems of individuals. Staff are viewed as an expense for the organization and staff development and training as a means of solving problems. Human resource management, in contrast, stresses the proactive, developmental management of people as a major resource for the achievement of organizational objectives. Staff development and training is an investment in that resource.

Cowling and Mailer outline a range of tasks or approaches, which make up human resource management.[4] These include human resource planning, recruitment and selection, appraisal, organizational development and design, and staff development and training. It is a portfolio of interconnected activities combined in a planned approach. Links are emphasized between human resource management and the management of rapid change. The concept of a human resource strategy by which required staff numbers and skills, now and for the future, are assessed and acquired through recruitment, training and development, provides the means by which the development of the individual, the workforce and the organization are linked to produce an effective response to change. The principle that training staff for their jobs and developing them for future roles is central to present and future levels of institutional performance and is found in the training literature of the last decade.

Links between staff and organizational development and between training and the other human resource management functions are also stressed. Thus, another set of issues emerges. In addition to the question of whether the staff development and training function is systematically managed, there is the further question of whether it forms part of an integrated, systematic approach to human resource management which is itself closely related to library and institutional planning and management.

One indicator of such an approach is the appointment of a senior member of library staff with responsibility for human resource management. A recent article records the emergence of a few examples of this role in the new universities.[5] In contrast, American university libraries have had posts with titles such as 'Personnel Librarian' since the 1970s. Current practice in relation to the development and training of American academic library staff is reviewed in the penultimate chapter. The final chapter comments on themes and issues raised throughout the book and draws conclusions for the future.

It may be helpful to end by explaining the definitions which are assumed throughout the book. 'Staff development' is taken to mean:

> A purposive effort intended to strengthen the library's capability to fulfil its mission effectively and efficiently by encouraging and providing for the growth of its human resources.[6]

'Training' is understood as:

> The process by which an individual learns new ways, information or techniques and changes from a state of being incapable of doing the job or being ineffective.[7]

The two together encompass all the means by which staff are enabled to do their present jobs effectively and to prepare themselves to meet changing needs.

Where the term 'new' university/ies is used, this refers to those institutions which changed from polytechnic to university status in 1992. The term 'old' universities includes all those universities which had that status prior to 1992.

Finally, 'academic libraries' are understood to include those in universities and higher and further education colleges. While further education college libraries may differ in size from the others, the influences upon them are essentially the same, as are the resulting issues. It is also understood that academic libraries are frequently part of converged services, which may have a wide range of different titles.

References

1 Joint Funding Councils' Libraries Review Group, *Report*, Bristol, HEFCE, 1993, 34–5.
2 Fielden Consultancy, *Supporting expansion: a report on human resource management in academic libraries, for the Joint Funding Councils' Libraries Review Group*, Bristol, HEFCE, 1993, 45.
3 Fielden Consultancy, *op. cit.*, 37.
4 Cowling, Alan and Mailer, Chloe, *Managing human resources*, 2nd. edn, London, Edward Arnold, 1990, 73.
5 Oldroyd, Margaret, 'The role of the staff development and training manager

in the new universities, *British journal of academic librarianship*, **9** (3), 1994, 201–8.

6 Conroy, Barbara, *Library staff development and continuing education: principles and practices*, Littleton, Colorado, Libraries Unlimited, 1978, XV.

7 Blanksby, Margaret, *Staff training*, Newcastle-upon-Tyne, Association of Assistant Librarians, 1988, 1.

Reference 1 above is a full citation for the Follett Report and reference 2 is a full citation for the Fielden Report. In subsequent lists of references, they are abbreviated to 'Follett Report' and 'Fielden Report' respectively.

1

The University Staff Development Context

PROFESSOR PATRICIA PARTINGTON

Introduction

Staff development and training for all groups of staff in higher education is more extensively provided in the 1990s than at any previous stage of its development. Nonetheless, compared with investment in staff by other large organizations, universities and colleges still have some way to go in (a) the level of resource they devote to this area, (b) the recognition accorded to its importance and potential, and (c) linking planning for staff development explicitly to institutional and departmental planning. It has been identified as an area of key strategic importance by enlightened leaders within higher education and presented as such at international conferences.

> Strategic management by individual institutions is the key to a generalised process of change in Europe . . . It must be based on leadership, vision, communication and evaluation, both inside and outside the establishment. It requires, furthermore, a greater flexibility of organisation in order to enhance the capacity and willingness of all concerned to innovate and contribute to the achievement of institutional policies. Finally, it needs, as part of the institution's human resources development policy, much greater emphasis on the management training of officers, deans and heads of department.[1]

This chapter aims to give detail of (a) the changes in higher education which have led to increased emphasis on and provision of staff development; (b) the background to staff development and training in UK higher education; (c) the current state of staff development for all groups of staff including reference to specific examples of programmes for library staff, and (d) suggestions of future development in the provision of HE training and development.

Changes in higher education

Higher education institutions within the UK and beyond have been and are a focus of wide-ranging and rapid changes. The sources of influence for these changes are numerous and varied: political, social, economic, educational, epistemological, legal, technological. The changes explored in this section have profound implications for staffing issues and the professional development of all groups of staff in higher education.

The changing resource base and allocation systems

The economic climate has affected levels of public funding for education and has led to: (a) the creation of more selective and rigorous systems of informing the allocation mechanisms of such funds, and (b) greater diversity of funding sources. These differing patterns of funding have an impact on the recruitment, employment conditions, and management and professional development of staff. Internal devolution of management responsibilities for financial planning and budgeting has led, for example, to increasing requests for programmes of financial management development from all groups of staff.

More robust accountability at all levels

With the tightening of the public purse has come a strengthening of accountability: from funding bodies to Government at one level, and from the individual staff member to his/her peer or senior colleague at another. These accountability measures impose a new set of priorities on the knowledge and range of skills which staff must possess and display. This again has implications for various aspects of higher education practice. What kind of management structures should be in place to ensure speedy and effective responses to initiatives? What kind of staff skills are needed to support those responses? Such questions are currently posed in all' areas of universities and colleges – from libraries and administrative areas to academic departments.

Demonstration rather than assumption of excellence

A central aim of universities and colleges has been and continues to be the pursuit of excellence in their individually targeted areas of activity. Until the 1980s only partial and un-coordinated evidence had been expected from HEIs to indicate that they were achieving the excellence they sought. Now the funding councils' cyclical research assessment exercises, the quality assessment procedures for evaluating educational provision in subject areas, the work of the Higher Education Quality Council (HEQC) together with the continuing accreditation activities of professional and statutory bodies combine to form a more extensive and systematic, but arguably not yet coherent, approach to the assurance of the quality of academic practice. The achievement of excellence or even competence in all core activities is no longer assumed, but must be demonstrated and evaluated. All staff including, crucially, library staff, are involved in supporting the educational and research practices of HEIs, and need to be developed to respond to the above processes.

The relationship with Government

Recently Government Departments have exerted substantial influence on the ways in which the central activities of universities and colleges are conducted and managed. The Department for Education and Employment, through the higher education funding councils, relates funding for both research and teaching to performance criteria and quality measures designed and operated by those councils. The former Employment Department's role increased in significance in parallel with the greater influence of employers on universities and through projects such as the Enterprise in Higher Education Initiative.[2] The Government's Cabinet Office and its Citizen's Charter Unit introduced the Higher Education Charter[3] which was intended to be followed by the implementation of local charters within every higher education institution. These focus on the notion of 'consumer satisfaction', and set out a series of obligations for the institution in respect of all its consumers: students, research contractors, employers, members of the local community etc.

These influences on universities have led to a change in culture within many, where each department is regarded and operated as a market-led 'business', where the 'consumer' is an influential force, and where competition is highly significant and arguably, collegiality is undermined and undervalued. These changed values and consequent practices have led to a reconsideration of the roles and tasks of staff in both academic and academic-related areas, and in turn to questions of their management and development.

The influence of employers and other organizations

The involvement of Government has also included pressures on universities and colleges to engage with commercial, industrial and other public sector employers for a variety of purposes, for example: (a) funding for research, development, and projects associated with the enhancement of teaching and learning; and (b) involvement of employers in partnerships in both research and teaching. Increased involvement with organizations in these ways has led to the consideration by universities of external management models and practices and to the analysis of their appropriateness for higher education.[4] Government, through the DFEE, has encouraged this investigation further by funding studies of management and leadership in higher education with reference to management in other sectors.[5]

An additional consequence of the influence of employers on university operations has been a greater knowledge within higher education of the variety and flexibility of employment contracts, conditions of service and working practices across diverse organizations. This has had the effect of opening up considerably the previously rather narrow and traditional employment practices within higher education, and has involved, for example, the introduction of staff appraisal schemes and in some cases performance-related pay. All these changes have had considerable impact on staff development policy and delivery. Notably, university librarians became involved early on in the design of appraisal schemes appropriate to their work, e.g. University of Sheffield Library.[6]

The impact of technological developments on academic and management practices

It is evident that technological developments in computing, networking and satellite transmission have had and will continue to have a far-reaching impact on academic and management practices in higher education. There are extensive implications for the continuing professional development of staff, which have hitherto not been fully acknowledged. The full potential of the advanced information systems now available is arguably not being exploited in the majority of universities and colleges because of a failure of managements

to recognize (a) that potential, and (b) the staff development requirements and resources to utilize it fully.

Greater diversity of student entry

The expansion of student entry in the 1990s has been characterized
by greater diversity of students – widening international student
intake, increased numbers of mature students, both full-time and
part-time, and students with non-traditional entry qualifications.
This diversity has resulted in the need for new approaches to the
management of learning, for example, new course structures and
teamwork approaches to teaching which incorporate staff such as
librarians and technicians, as well as academics. Again, these developments raise issues of (a) contractual arrangements for staff, and (b)
training and professional development of all staff involved.

The results of these changes: the requirements of staff and managers

All the preceding changes combine to result in the following requirements of a variety of levels of staff and in all staff groups within
higher education institutions:

  (i) their engagement in strategic planning at institutional,
       departmental and individual levels;
 (ii) their involvement in devolved management of all resources;
(iii) their responses to accountability measures, such as research
       and educational quality assessment;
 (iv) the development of their capabilities to respond to a larger
       and more diverse student intake;
  (v) the enhancement of teaching and learning strategies;
 (vi) their increased engagement with industry and commerce in
       both research and teaching;
(vii) their willingness and capability to acknowledge the benefits
       of, and to use new technologies;
(viii) the development of 'consumer satisfaction' approaches;
 (ix) their pursuance of effective fund-raising opportunities;
  (x) their acceptance of new employment contracts and conditions
       of service, including innovations such as staff appraisal;

(xi)   their recognition of the need for continuing regular review of their activities and practices leading to evaluation, re-planning and changed approaches;

(xii)   and finally, underpinning all of the above, the acknowledgement of their own individual and departmental needs of continuing, career-long, professional development.

The development of staff training in universities/colleges

In response to the above changes and their implications, provision of staff development at various levels – from local (within institutions) through to international – has markedly increased in the late 1980s and 1990s. Key processes and reports which have supported this progress have been:

- greater emphasis on efficiency in university management;[4]
- the introduction of staff appraisal systems from 1987 onwards;
- the work of the Committee of Vice-Chancellors and Principals (CVCP) and The Universities Committee for Non-Teaching Staffs (UCNS) groups under the chairmanship of Professor Brian Fender;[7, 8]
- the quality assurance processes – the development of academic audit and funding council assessment;
- the cyclical research assessment exercises, and the publication of the Office for Science and Technology White Paper, *Realising our potential*.[9]

The background to the current state of staff development in UK universities and colleges is traced now through these important phases in respect of all staff groups in universities.

Academic staff development

National bodies and regional networks

The Committee of Vice-Chancellors and Principals (CVCP) has had a coordinating role in academic staff development since 1972 when it instituted a Coordinating Committee for the Training of University Teachers (CCTUT) with a part-time national Coordinating Officer. His/her role was (a) to organize national conferences on behalf of CCTUT, (b) to undertake surveys, such as the one by Dr George Brown which led to the formulation in 1987 of the CVCP's *Code of practice on academic staff training*,[10] and (c) to issue other publications, for example, *Staff development matters*.[11] The work of the CCTUT and that of the CVCP's national coordinator was later in 1989 continued through UCoSDA (initially named USDTU – The Universities' Staff Development and Training Unit now entitled The Universities' and Colleges' Staff Development Agency), whose work is described later in this chapter.

Additionally the Committee of Scottish Higher Education Principals (COSHEP) has a long and indeed strong involvement in supporting academic and other staff development through its Staff Development Coordinating Committee. This has high profile membership from each Scottish HEI and has sub-committees which focus on particular areas, such as the Teaching, Learning and Research and the Management Sub-Committees.

The former polytechnics' central organization of directors/principals, the Committee of Directors of Polytechnics (CDP), introduced in the 1980s its own training unit with a limited life-span and the principal, short-term objective of organizing professional development programmes to support polytechnic staff through the changes brought about by incorporation.

Some national subject associations have a commendable record of professional development for research and for teaching, e.g. The British Psychological Society.[12] The Research Councils, notably the Economic and Social Research Council (ESRC) and Engineering and Physical Sciences Research Council (EPSRC), have also demonstrated increasing interest in professional preparation for academics in their research activities. Alongside these are two professional membership associations at national level which organize conferences and publications in support of staff development and training in academic practice. The Society for Research into Higher Education (SRHE) is a recognized international research organization which mounts a prominent annual conference and provides an extensive collection of publications focused on higher education developments. The Staff and Educational Development Association (SEDA) encourages networking for the enhancement of teaching and learning through its primary focus on organizing staff development conferences and workshops. It also publishes and disseminates a journal, *The new academic*, along with regular publications on educational development.

Its most recent contribution to the improvement of teaching quality has been its teacher accreditation scheme,[13] through which institutions' own development programmes might be externally accredited.

As is usually associated with such national bodies, regional groupings have emerged across the UK which have had considerable influence on the progress of staff development in individual institutions. These exist now in most regions and each provides a varied programme of events to which institutions might send their staff. Examples of the longest established and most vibrant of such academic staff development regional networks are: in Scotland, supported by COSHEP; in the Midlands – the M1/M69 link – organized by universities in the vicinity of those motorways; and the SEDA supported northern and southern educational development groups.

Local provision

Every higher education institution now has a coordinator or a coordinating team (of varying size) to provide opportunities for professional development. The point has now been reached when an academic on entry to the profession can expect to be offered preparation and training for his/her role, although the scale of what is on offer still varies considerably and programmes are also regularly offered to more senior staff. Three important developments in the 1980s contributed to this current position. Firstly, the establishment of the Jarratt Committee by the CVCP, which investigated and reported on the management efficiency of the 'old' universities, led to the significantly increased provision of management development programmes for senior academic staff. Secondly, the introduction – as part of the salary negotiations between the Association of University Teachers (AUT) and the CVCP in 1987 – of staff appraisal schemes for academic and related staff in the old universities emphasized the need for staff development to respond to identified requirements. This was subsequently followed by the introduction of appraisal schemes in the new universities. Finally, the emphasis on quality assurance, the planning and introduction of academic audit in the late 1980s and then quality assessment has led to the enhancement of teacher training programmes in universities and colleges right across the UK.

The Council for National Academic Awards (CNAA), the awarding body for polytechnic degrees, throughout its existence also exerted influence on local staff development activities and developed its quality enhancement role during the 1980s in support of these. The role of staff and student associations at both local and national levels must also be acknowledged for the continuing emphasis they have placed on provision of staff development for their members.

Academic-related and administrative staff development

In 1972, in parallel with its establishment of the CCTUT, the CVCP inaugurated its Administrative Staff Training Committee and appointed a national coordinator for administrative training. This person's tasks included the organization of national programmes of training, and the encouragement and continuing support of regional networks to provide complementary training to the national events. Although this work focused very largely on course provision, an impressive volume of training materials was also compiled and circulated across the universities in support of local activities. By the 1980s, a well coordinated training framework was in place across the UK, which provided for administrators at key career stages – induction, middle grade and senior staff – and which continues still.[14, 15] These developments owed much of their success to the consistently strong support of Registrars and Secretaries individually and collectively through their national group, the Conference of Registrars and Secretaries (CRS, now AHUA – the Association of Heads of University Administration).

The national professional bodies/associations for the various academic-related staff groups have also played a large part in furthering professional development. The former polytechnic and university library staff organizations – COPOL and SCONUL – have concentrated considerable effort on training activities and their support, and have worked with the Library Association on training matters. Similarly the AUA (Association for University Administrators) has consistently provided programmes of staff development

The regional groupings for administrative staff development, set up by the CVCP's national coordinator, operate right across the UK in five areas: the Midlands, Northern, Scottish, Southern and Welsh regions. They function most commonly on a reciprocal basis by establishing an organizing committee made up of a representative from each member university, which plans and delivers a programme of events provided at a minimum cost by each of the universities involved.

Staff development and training for university and college professional staff remains unevenly provided for at local level, despite the commendable developments and support nationally. In those institutions where the Head of Administration, Director of Personnel and other heads (a) place value on it and (b) devote resources to it, significant opportunities exist. However, the onus is often still very much on individual staff members to press their own case for training, and the tendency remains then for them to be offered an external short course to cater in an *ad hoc* way for an immediate need. Coherent, career-long, in-house pathways of development are still few and far between.

Allied staff development

Included in this designation, 'allied', are all the other support staff who are responsible for the smooth functioning of universities and colleges, and whose development has long been relatively poorly resourced.[16] The main agents at national and local levels for encouraging better training opportunities for allied staff have been the trades unions, notably the Managerial, Scientific and Financial Trade Union (MSF), the National Union of Public Employees (NUPE) and UNISON. As early as the 1960s, for example, MSF (then ASTMS) urged, in its negotiations with CVCP, for systematic training to be in place for university technical staff, and took a strong interest through its local branches in the development of well coordinated trainee technician programmes. The Universities' Committee for Non-Teaching Staff (UCNS) of the CVCP, the central body which dealt with employment matters for allied staff, gave support to the development of training by instituting a central training sub-committee and a series of regional UCNS committees which also supported regionally-based training activities.

The UCNS, through the work of the two 'Fender Committees', further supported the progress of training for allied staff through the two reports, *Investing in people* and *Promoting people*. The other three groups of allied staff which have benefited from coordinated training approaches have been secretarial, catering and library support staff.

Librarians, in many cases, have seen their total staff complement as a team providing an academic service to the university community, and have consequently provided training for all staff as appropriate. It is not surprising, therefore, that the strongest interest within universities in the development of 'Investors in People', a national initiative emanating from the former Employment Department,[17] has come from libraries and from commercial, residential and catering areas.

The current state of staff development

The preceding brief overview of the progress of staff development for all staff in universities during the 1970s and 1980s has indicated: (a) gradually increasing but uneven provision, which has been focused on staff categories rather than functions or tasks, and (b) a strong tendency for staff development to be seen as attendance at short courses 'bolted on' when necessary. During the period described, there was little appreciation of the notion of career-long, continuing professional development related to both institutional and individual goals.

Currently we are at the threshold of the next phase of strategically planned and more fully resourced activity, and several factors have influenced this: greater recognition by university and college managements of professional development as a key factor in effecting change, the impact of the external quality assurance bodies for research and teaching, and the work of national bodies, such as UCoSDA, in promoting the value of professional development and supplying services in its support.

The Universities' and Colleges' Staff Development Agency (UCoSDA)

The planning and establishment in 1989 of UCoSDA as a central resource to support local staff development and training represented a significant step forward in several respects. First, the acknowledgement of the activity by Vice-Chancellors and Principals as one which deserved national support emphasized its importance. Secondly, the fact that the first three years of funding for the agency came from the UGC (University Grants Committee) signalled that the funding body for higher education also recognized the crucial importance of staff development. Thirdly, the remit of the agency presented a new model which took the concept of staff development forward to that of an essential, strategic component of institutional development. The key features of its remit were that:

(a) it was to act as a national resource centre offering primarily consultancy, advice and the production of materials to support local staff development, rather than as a course-providing agency;

(b) it was only to offer conferences, seminars etc., to appropriate groupings (those small enough to be cost-effective and professionally desirable at national level such as Vice-Chancellors, Pro-Vice-Chancellors, Heads of University Administration and beginning administrators etc.) and to staff developers themselves in support of their own professional development;

(c) it was to provide a service in respect of all staff groups and, where possible, to encourage a functional rather than staff category approach to development activities;

(d) through its materials and publications it was to promote a broader interpretation of development and training to incorporate a spectrum of activities from independent and work-based learning through to departmental development activities;

(e) it was to encourage professional development related to career development and linked closely with the newly introduced staff appraisal schemes as the mechanisms for identifying individual staff development needs;

(f) it was to promote the importance of staff development and training as a key component in ensuring the capacity of departments and institutions as a whole to achieve their missions and objectives.

These remain the guiding principles underpinning the work of UCoSDA, as is evident in its most recent brochure of services.[18]

Current local provision

This concept of a central resource offering consultancy and materials support to member institutions has provided a model for universities and colleges which is currently highly appropriate to their own staff development units. With devolved management structures and the impact of subject-focused quality procedures for research and teaching, the local staff developer's role has changed in recent times to involve advisory services to specific departments and schools in their responses to external monitoring and regulation. Heads of Schools now operate much more clearly as leaders and managers of their resources and of their staff, and have a significant staff development responsibility, for which advice and guidance is increasingly sought from the central staff development service. Innovations in teaching, pressures to secure funding for research and to publish research, as well as developments in administrative and management practices, have all combined to require of the staff development office in universities a comprehensive, institution-wide menu of programmes – in addition to the enhanced level of departmental advisory work. For all these reasons, the 1990s have seen (a) an expansion in the personnel involved in the staff and educational development function, and (b) a diversity of models emerging to provide it.

Across universities and colleges a wide range of structures exists to support and coordinate staff and educational development, ranging from (a) those affiliated to an academic faculty, to (b) those which reside within the personnel function, to (c) those which are independent departments, in some cases deriving from an externally pump-primed initiative, such as Enterprise in Higher Education. An overview of models currently in existence is explored and their relative advantages and disadvantages analysed in UCoSDA Green Paper Ten.[19]

The task force of members who compiled this Green Paper[20] drawn from HEIs across the UK, identified the following current trends in university professional development provision, after reviewing the position in some 30 universities:

- centrally designed and directed initiatives, increasingly linked to institutional objectives and priorities (for instance, equal opportunities developments, quality initiatives, staff development services to support CPD, common IT training etc.);
- the emergence of institution-wide schemes for professional development, embracing all staff categories (both academic and support/allied staff) – with all HEIs now having at least one designated person in place with responsibility for this function;

- greater emphasis on professional development for teaching and learning, and the gradual introduction of incentive schemes to recognize and reward excellence in teaching;
- linkage of staff development to appraisal and personal career development planning, including the use of portfolios;
- a recognition of the need to plan more effectively for continuing professional development by making specific allocations within the organization's economy, e.g. a percentage of total revenue budget dedicated to staff development and training, or a defined amount of time which every member of staff is expected to spend in participation in staff development activities;
- the extension of professional development support activities to include in-house work provided by, for example, Schools of Education and Business/Management Departments;
- a growing awareness of the importance of CPD information and records, accredited qualifications and portability of recognized learning achievements through assignment and transfer of credit.

Universities are increasingly looking to the design and/or adoption of transferable, portable qualification routes which will place professional development within a clearly structured framework of accredited awards offered at appropriate career levels, including:

- in-house awards, often credit-rated as part of professional development programmes;
- awards offered by other organizations/institutions (including other HEIs) which staff may follow;
- accredited awards of professional bodies;
- Scottish/National Vocational Qualifications.

Training and development for library staff

In respect of library staff, in particular at national and local levels, the Follett and Fielden reports and their implications will increasingly influence provision for their professional development. UCoSDA has been involved with the Standing Conference of National and University Libraries (SCONUL) during 1994/95 in a creative new senior management development initiative based at the Aston Business School. This intensive, consecutive 12-day programme, including attendance over a weekend, had a strategic management focus and included components on the management of all key resources, as well as the role of the senior library manager in contributing to the strategic planning and development of the institution as a whole. This emphasis on integrated, collaborative senior management was directly in line with the first of Fielden's recommendations. This programme was mounted for the first time in March/April, 1995 and attracted strong interest and the projected number of applicants. It is in process of being organized again during 1996 and is expected to remain equally attractive to senior library staff.

UCoSDA's work over the past six years on the development and implementation of staff appraisal schemes and their relationship to staff training has influenced developments in university libraries. The University of Sheffield Library's appraisal scheme and training pack was developed with reference to the then USDTU's guidelines and materials, and librarians in several universities have attended seminars at local, regional and national levels on staff appraisal skills, run by UCoSDA advisers. Such schemes have led to more systematic identification of the training needs of all library personnel, both professional and support staff, and therefore to better informed staff development planning.

UCoSDA's work in conjunction with the Employment Department concerning (a) the development of S/NVQs as accreditation routes, and (b) the implementation of 'Investors in People', has found a ready audience in senior library staff. 'Investors in People' as a framework for the encouragement of strategic staff development and training linked to the library's goals and objectives and to those of the university/college as a whole is being considered increasingly seriously by a number of librarians.

Future development in provision

What is needed now for all staff in universities and colleges, irrespective of their particular category, is a continuous career development programme based on:

(a) systematic, regular means of identifying professional development needs, e.g. staff appraisal, mentoring etc;

(b) a personal development planning process instituted and encouraged by senior and departmental managers and carried out by mentors and/or appraisers;

(c) coherent and coordinated initial and continuing professional development (CPD) programmes based primarily on functions and roles, rather than on staff categories;

(d) logs or portfolios which record individuals' professional development and training;

(e) the availability of accredited qualification programmes as appropriate for all personnel in higher education.

The final section of this chapter briefly explores these five proposals.

Policies and strategies

The hierarchies and values in universities have combined to keep people 'in their proper station'. The suspicion is not that staff have been badly managed but that they have been inappropriately managed. The need now is to develop ways in which the full potential of every individual can be identified and developed. All managers have a teaching role – a responsibility to stimulate learning by their staff. Involvement in their own learning is the most important condition for ensuring staff development.[21]

Several interconnecting strands are identified in this quotation, namely: management commitment, involvement, identification, support and cultures enabling opportunity. Effective CPD requires each of these to be addressed openly, coherently and specifically in system-wide, institutional and departmental policies and strategies – in essence, these items must be at the heart of institutional polices relating to staff and they must be translated into effective practice in departments.

That agenda may be pursued through incorporation of these issues in the strategic plan and integration of them within the operational culture of an institution. The latter is essential, but neither will ensure commitment from all stakeholders unless effective ways are developed of addressing needs at various levels, signalling clearly that effective development is important and that leaders and managers attach a high priority to it and actively involve individuals in the development processes and practices.

Ways and means

The translation of policy into practice should be informed by the views of participants and also by lessons from research and experience. Effective audits of development needs with inputs from individuals and their appraisers, mentors and managers will contribute to successful and appreciated strategies and programmes. Partnerships, both inter- and intra-institutional and of varying size and complexity, are likely to offer creative avenues for effective marriages of interests and expertise. Many examples of such partnerships exist in networks and consortia but there is considerable scope for further development and deepening of this approach.

The five specific ways and means mentioned initially in this section for developing CPD programmes for all staff rest upon the prerequisite that the need for CPD of staff in HEIs is accepted by all stakeholders, is expected of each individual, is resourced and is evaluated. These are vital ingredients of the enhancement which may be required in institutional policies and strategies.

A six-step cyclical model of CPD for all staff is shown in the following figure.[22]

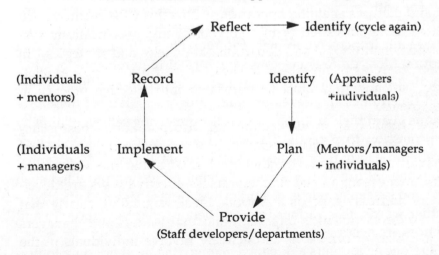

Fig. 1.1 *Cyclical Model of Continuing Professional Development*

The process starts with the identification of needs for training and development, leading on to a planning process supported by mentors and managers, which incorporates consideration of both personal development planning and departmental/unit staff development plans. This is followed by coherent provision of the desired CPD, which individuals then put into practice (implementation). Simultaneously they also record their CPD through portfolios or logs. The initial phase of the process ends with reflection which feeds into the identification of further needs in the continuing career-long CPD of each staff member. The pace of the process will vary from person to person. Often the apparently smooth continuing procedure will experience turbulence because of job change or some other discontinuity, for example, a requirement to develop new skills, to re-train, to acquire new competences, to gain qualifications, etc.

The formal requirement of CPD – issues to be addressed

The thrust of this chapter has been that CPD is an essential rather than a desirable objective, an obligation rather than an option; it is both a professional expectation and duty and a responsibility which institutions have for their professionals (which in higher education means all staff). Two crucial words, formal and professional, do not conform with prevailing cultures or practices in higher education. Staff in HEIs, academics in particular, prefer freedom to regulation and are apt to perceive formal requirements as intrusions into that freedom. Most professions now have formal requirements for CPD, including the need to record the specific experiences within designated timeframes and developmental categories. Many of these professions guard their autonomy carefully, preferring self-regulation by the profession to potential intrusion from external controls. These precedents lead to the conclusion that formal CPD could be accepted within the culture and practices of higher education provided such provision is seen as relevant, supportive, progressive and effective – in other words, that various interests believe that the processes and practices are necessary and beneficial.

Here one encounters a dilemma, namely the need not only to persuade through arguments but also, if possible, to illustrate benefits and demonstrate effectiveness; the dilemma is that illustration and demonstration tend to require evidence from implementation, and implementation requires both commitment to and policies for particular strategies and practices. Fortunately, few human systems are in a uniform state of development, so it is often possible to use illustrations from elsewhere to add evidence to arguments for changes to policies and practices.

Similar tensions exist in CPD between the generic and the specific needs for training and development. Because we like to be recognized as individuals, most of us have a preference for things to be tailored to our needs, wishes or expectations. That generalization certainly applies to attitudes to staff development. Thus formal CPD will need to incorporate considerable flexibility (capability for 'tailoring') in order to meet the varied and changing needs of individuals. Here the tension is to satisfy that necessity within a coherent framework – a tension potentially sharpened by the demands for accreditation. In part, the solution might appear to be in the adoption of higher level Scottish/National Vocational Qualifications (S/NVQs) as the means of accrediting formal CPD, (a) because these are work-related and work-based and (b) because of the considerable flexibility which is an integral feature of that framework. However, as the UCoSDA feasibility study for the Employment Department[23] revealed, higher education institutions remain to be convinced about the appropriateness of these qualifications. Moreover, the attempts by the project team to match various categories of CPD need in HEIs to existing recognized S/NVQ strands revealed significant mismatches and gaps, suggesting that further development would be required before widespread adoption by HEIs would be practicable or prudent. Given these difficulties, some might question the need to accredit CPD. The benefits principally rest in assuring the quality of the practices and provisions, and offering a meaningful framework for individuals and employers, for recording CPD. Arguably these are essential ingredients for effective learning by staff in organizations where the principal pursuit is learning and which ought, therefore, to be operating as 'learning organizations'.

References

1   Commission of European Communities, *Higher education in the European Community: towards the year 2000*, Rome, CEC, 1991.
2   Gray, H., *Changing higher education: going with the grain*, Sheffield, UCoSDA,

University of Salford and KPMG, 1995.

3 Department For Education, *Higher quality and choice: The Charter for Higher Education*, London, HMSO, 1993.

4 Jarratt, A., *The Jarratt Committee report on efficiency studies in universities*, London, CVCP, 1985.

5 Middlehurst, R., *Changing roles of university leaders and managers*, Sheffield, USDU, 1991.

6 University of Sheffield Library, *Staff appraisal at the University of Sheffield: guidelines for appraisers and appraisees in the University Library*, Sheffield, University of Sheffield Library, 1990.

7 Fender, B., *Report of the Fender Committee: investing in people*, London, CVCP, 1987.

8 Fender, B., *Promoting people: a strategic framework for the management and development of staff in UK universities*, London, CVCP, 1993.

9 Office for Science and Technology, *White Paper: Realising our potential*, London, HMSO, Cm 2250, 1993.

10 Brown, G. A., *Academic staff development code of practice*, London, CVCP, 1987.

11 Matheson, C. C., *Staff development matters*, Loughborough, Quorn Selective Repro. Ltd., 1981.

12 UCoSDA, *Guidelines for assessment of the PhD in psychology and related disciplines*, Sheffield, UCoSDA and The British Psychological Society, 1995.

13 SEDA, *The accreditation of teachers in universities*, 2nd. edn, Birmingham, SEDA, 1995.

14 Guildford, P., *Staff development provision in universities of the United Kingdom*, Sheffield, UCoSDA, 1990.

15 Guildford, P., *Briefing Paper No 16: Training and development for university administrators: a position/discussion paper*, Sheffield, UCoSDA, 1995.

16 Hardwick, R., *Green Paper No 7: Approaches towards the improvement of support/allied staff development*, Sheffield, UCoSDA, 1994

17 Whiteley, T., *Briefing Paper No 2: Investors in people*, Sheffield, UCoSDA, 1993.

18 UCoSDA, *Information about membership benefits*, Sheffield, UCoSDA, 1995.

19 Partington, P. A., *Green Paper No 10: Continuing professional development for staff in higher education*, Sheffield, UCoSDA, 1994.

20 Partington P. A., *op. cit.*, 19.

21 Fender, B., *op. cit.*, 8.

22 Gordon, G. and Partington, P. A., *Emerging agendas and frameworks for staff development*, Zurich, EAIR Conference, 1995.

23 UCoSDA, *A feasibility study on the application of higher level N/SVQs to staff development in higher education*, Sheffield, UCoSDA, 1994.

2

Continuing Professional Development

JULIE PARRY

Remember: learning is a life-long process. In the fast-changing 21st century, only fools will ever consider their education complete.[1]

Introduction

As in many other professions, it is now formally recognized that those who work in the field of library and information services must commit themselves to ongoing development throughout their working lives. In days when the pace of change was more leisurely it was standard practice to base a career on the firm foundation of a good library school education. Indeed, professional education is still essential to provide qualified staff with a broad theoretical understanding of information management and a range of basic transferable skills. However, there are now a number of factors that influence the need for staff at all levels to continue developing their skills and knowledge as outlined in the first chapter.

Terminology

During the 1980s, the term continuing education was commonly used to denote the updating of professional skills and knowledge. At that time, Jones and Jordan noted that there was less distinction in the United Kingdom than in the United States between the use of the terms staff development and continuing education;[2] 'continuing professional development' (CPD) was the phrase adopted by Royston Brown in a report that led to the establishment of the Library Association's (LA) *Framework for continuing professional development*. Although CPD is now the preferred term in the literature, anecdotal evidence suggests that staff are still often unable to distinguish meaningfully between staff development, training and CPD.

Scope

In fact, CPD is a broad concept that includes staff development, training and personal development. It is characterized by a systematic approach to assessing needs, undertaking training or development activities and monitoring outcomes. The LA has cited the following definition, which is also used by other occupational groups:

> The systematic maintenance, improvement and broadening of knowledge and skills and the development of personal qualities necessary for the execution of professional and technical duties throughout the practitioner's working life.[3]

Training and development have been defined in the introduction. Personal development extends beyond immediate training needs and encourages a wider and longer view of the needs of individuals. Enlightened institutions recognize the benefits that arise from having staff who are committed to their own personal development. More cynical employers may be reluctant to commit resources in order to develop staff who might then leave for better jobs.

The importance of CPD

Beleaguered librarians trying to maintain services in the face of growing pressure from students, academic staff and management might expect to be forgiven for putting the development of people lower down the agenda than the development of services, systems and structures. However, one thing that these three elements have in common is people. Even the most automated libraries need people to manage systems, to carry out data entry and to help users, all of which require different skills that must be regularly updated. Finding time for staff development activities is notoriously difficult, perhaps even more difficult than acquiring training funds or choosing appropriate trainers. But if staff have no opportunity to develop their own abilities, then services, systems and structures are likely to stagnate and will soon fail to meet the demands made upon them.

Benefits for employers

Clearly, ongoing training is necessary to enable staff to keep up to date with changes. In a responsive service, processes and procedures will be constantly monitored and modified to meet changing needs. Managers and supervisors need to ensure that all staff understand new procedures and are able to put them into practice. Employees who are used to assessing their own development needs are more likely to be able to work in partnership with others to identify training needs and to be creative in meeting those needs. Individuals who take a positive attitude towards their own learning and development often display confidence in challenging the status quo and suggesting solutions to problems. Organizations with a strong reputation for supporting CPD may find that they attract new high-calibre recruits who are drawn by the ethos of the institution. At the same time, a high-quality CPD programme can enable an institution to develop its own staff so that they are well equipped to take advantage of internal opportunities for promotion.

Benefits for individuals

The benefits for individuals range from the purely practical to the rather more intangible factors that contribute to motivation and job satisfaction. At the level of basic training most people find that learning how to do a job properly aids effectiveness and efficiency. For example, a well-trained online searcher will be able to conduct searches without constantly having to resort to the manuals and will know how to exploit short-cuts to good effect. Each search is likely to follow a recognized pattern and yield useful results. Inadequately trained searchers are more likely to suffer frustration at their inability to achieve the best results and to spend a lot of time trying to get to grips with the system. The confidence that arises from the ability to do a job well can be highly motivating and has the added benefit of inspiring confidence in the academic staff or students for whom the service is being provided.

A structured approach to CPD enables staff to consider their long-term goals and to plan how to achieve them. A system such as the LA's *Framework for continuing professional development* encourages people to maintain a record of training and development activities, without which it is easy to forget just how much has been achieved over a period of time. Perhaps most importantly, staff can benefit enormously from a partnership approach to planning their development. Working closely with mentors and line managers can be of significant help in evolving strategies and gaining support.

Who needs CPD?

One of the recommendations of the Fielden Report was 'that the term 'professional' as applied to a particular grade of staff be abolished'.[4] Fielden made the point that all staff should be achieving the highest standards of professionalism in their services to customers of all kinds. The distinction is becoming increasingly blurred between tasks and responsibilities traditionally referred to as professional or non-professional. Cataloguing, once the sole preserve of the professionally qualified librarian, is increasingly an automated process undertaken by staff without formal qualifications or so-called paraprofessional staff. Qualified academic librarians are now involved in teaching and learning, exploiting IT and managing a whole range of resources. Furthermore, with the advent of S/NVQs and distance learning courses in librarianship and information science there will be ample opportunities for staff at all levels to upgrade their skills and gain new qualifications. There are no defensible reasons why CPD opportunities should not be available to all, regardless of grade or pattern of work.

Different people – different needs

National trends towards part-time work and differing patterns of employment are mirrored in academic libraries. Opening hours are being extended in response to vociferous demands from students who may themselves be studying part-time. Organizations are seeking cost-effective ways of staffing service points and help-desks. A number of libraries employ qualified librarians and support staff specifically to work at weekends or during other periods when full-time staff are not available. The people who participate in job-shares or work unsocial hours generally seek such work because it enables them to continue with care responsibilities or to pursue other interests. They may do the job in order to keep their skills up to date or it might simply be a matter of needing the money. There may be staff who intend to return to work full-time and others who will never want more than a few hours' work each week.

Encouraging CPD activities under these circumstances provides quite a challenge for the manager. However, part-time staff will often be at the front-line of the service and users expect them to be as competent as any of their colleagues. A positive approach to development and the opportunity to participate in training activities will help to ensure that all staff are equipped to provide the highest standards of service to users. Timetabling can be particularly difficult and not many part-time staff are able to be totally flexible about their hours. Employers ought to provide what help they can, for example by offering to pay the cost of half a day's child-care to enable a member of staff to join an in-house training session.

The unwilling developer

Even the most enlightened organizations have staff who are not highly motivated and, even worse, tend to undermine the efforts of their colleagues. Negativity knows no bounds and cynicism about CPD can come from those who claim to be too old to learn anything new, too young to learn anything else, too senior to need any more development or too junior to do anything except follow orders. Forcing development on demotivated staff is not going to make them actually want to change, even if they grudgingly participate. A fairly long-term approach is necessary to establish a culture of trust and learning within which cynics can see for themselves the opportunities from which they could also benefit. At the same time, formal systems such as appraisal should be used to the full to identify training needs and to provide a forum for discussion about attitudes and personal development.

The unwilling employer

On the other hand, some staff find themselves working for an organization in which staff development is not valued and inadequate resources are committed to support CPD. An inability to recognize that good performance stems from good training and development may characterize a poor manager or head of service. It may be that the institutional decision-makers fail to understand that the most effective staff are those who are highly motivated and eager to apply a range of skills and knowledge in pursuit of common goals. Those who remain with such an organization, rather than leaving to develop their careers in a more supportive environment, need to demonstrate resilience and be assertive in taking responsibility for their own development.

Few employers are likely to respond positively to repeated complaints about lack of development opportunity or to staff who whine about the dreadfulness of everything. They are much more likely to be swayed by persuasive arguments about efficiency gains, improved performance and financial benefits. For example, the costs of poor recruitment decisions are well documented – from the human misery arising from poor working relationships to the financial implications of having to re-recruit after a failed probationary period. Anyone trying to persuade an employer that they would benefit from a course in recruitment would be well advised to stress the financial and human benefits to the organization from such an investment.

In the absence of any systematic institutional approach to training and development, individual staff would undoubtedly find the LA *Framework* invaluable. Staff who are committed to their own development should be seeking ways of effecting a cultural shift within their organization by raising awareness within the library service and, if possible, at senior management level.

Strategic management of CPD

The vital role of managers in structuring CPD is stressed by Sheila Corrall who points out that,

> Managers need to take a more holistic view of knowledge and skills requirements in relation to service priorities. They must also put in place the necessary infrastructure – a framework of policies, plans, programmes and procedures, enabling needs to be assessed systematically, activities to be recorded, and results to be evaluated and followed through in day-to-day activities. Finally, and arguably the most crucial and difficult issue, everyone must understand his or her own part in the process.[5]

Obviously, even managers who place a high value on development need to do considerably more than make encouraging noises and hand over funds for staff development activities. Otherwise, there is a danger that the most zealous individuals will want to spend a large proportion of their time undertaking all sorts of activities, many of which may be inappropriate or simply unnecessary. Meanwhile, their less purposeful colleagues may miss important opportunities and fail to reach their true potential.

Managers and individuals may have recourse to a number of systems to help them in managing effective staff development programmes.

Framework for Continuing Professional Development

The Library Association first published the *Framework* in 1992 and mailed a copy directly to each of its members. This initiative was welcomed by people who recognized the value of this approach to managing one's own professional development needs. However, there were many who failed to comprehend the significance of the document and a number who discarded it unopened. There was some initial support from committed employers who paid to become 'sponsoring employers' but the *Framework* has been generally greeted with indifference. Patrick Noon[6] has noted that 'the scheme's failure to establish itself as a credible professional tool stems partly from the growth of appraisal schemes which may obviate the need to use an entirely separate tool such as the *Framework*'. More worrying is Noon's assertion that 'no-one actually seems to be responsible for checking whether we have unwrapped our . . . *Framework* and, if they were, what would they do about it?'

It is regrettable that the *Framework* has not fired the imagination of more people. The scheme itself is commendable, although at first glance it can seem rather daunting. Closer examination reveals a carefully structured process that guides users systematically from an analysis of their present circumstances, through a detailed development plan to a personal record of qualifications, activities and responsibilities. Each step is clearly documented, enabling ideas to be refined and plans to be prioritized as the individual progresses through each stage.

The *Framework* is bound to appeal to people who already take a responsible attitude towards their own learning. Many others would be receptive given a little encouragement and practical guidance on how to get the best out of it. But as a voluntary scheme it is unlikely to gain widespread support without the active involvement of employers and managers. Human resource managers have much to gain from promoting the *Framework*, not as an alternative to appraisal but as a means of preparing for appraisal. The scheme offers the advantage of a more holistic approach in which individuals are encouraged to consider both professional and personal dimensions in establishing their own goals and objectives. People are actively encouraged to take decisions about their work and life rather than waiting passively for someone else to make things happen. For employers who choose to promote the *Framework* there could be tremendous potential in the combination of individual responsibility and management support, resulting in a harnessing of enthusiasm and the development of a flexible, skilled and motivated workforce.

The Library Association Charter

When Fielden suggested that the term 'professional' be abandoned, the word 'chartered' as a suitable alternative was not even considered. In many of the old universities, chartered status has traditionally been viewed as an irrelevance. Many job advertisements are aimed at chartered librarians but in many more it is a desirable rather than an essential characteristic and in a significant number it is ignored altogether. Nevertheless, to some people, chartership signifies a commitment to the profession and to one's personal and professional development. The view of Biddy Fisher[7] is that, 'The acquisition of Chartered status is a benchmark in the career of an information professional. Like a driving test, one can only start for real once it has been successfully achieved.' Certainly, Route A, the most common route to chartership, requires a structured training programme that lays a firm foundation for future CPD activities. In addition, the analytical approach required encourages a degree of self-awareness that can only be beneficial throughout the working life of any individual.

National Vocational Qualifications (NVQs)

NVQs and their Scottish equivalents, (SVQs), are qualifications based on the assessment of practical skills or competence. They are not tied to any particular type of course or training but focus on the ability of individuals to perform clearly identified tasks to a nationally agreed standard. Assessment is normally undertaken in the workplace and this has obvious implications for line managers who are expected to assess others. Indeed, there is a whole range of opportunities growing up for those who wish to gain NVQs from the Training and Development Lead Body in order to act as assessors and verifiers for library staff aiming to gain NVQs developed by the Information and Library Services (ILS) Lead Body.

Hazel Dakers[8] considers that the egalitarianism of NVQs makes them an attractive proposition, 'NVQs enable those who have not undergone traditional vocational education to be acknowledged for what they can do. For those who have been traditionally educated, NVQs are proof that they can do as well as know!' On the other hand, T. D. Wilson[9] argues strongly that the mechanistic approach of the NVQ framework benefits organizations at the expense of individuals. He contends that, at the higher level, NVQs will stifle the qualities of imagination, creativity, innovation and analytical thought 'that are the true competencies of the manager in any kind of organization'.

It is probably true that those who will benefit the most, in the short term, are staff who do not have formal library qualifications but who do have experience and responsibilities that deserve recognition. The challenge for academic libraries will be to establish appropriate procedures for assessment, whether within their own institutions or by using external assessment centres. Systematic training programmes will also be necessary both for assessors and for those seeking to gain NVQs. It is interesting to note that candidates for the City & Guilds Certificate for Library and Information Assistants now have to undertake a significant amount of workplace assessment in addition to the more traditional examinations.

Appraisal

The identification of training needs is a cornerstone of effective CPD and, ideally, responsibility for this should be shared between individuals and their managers. The LA *Framework* provides individuals with an excellent starting point for considering their own needs. Where an appraisal scheme is in operation, this is the ideal forum for discussing and documenting training needs. The best appraisal schemes relate staff development to performance and examine the contribution of the appraisee to wider organizational goals. In addition, there should be follow-up to ensure that agreed activities are actually happening and being evaluated. There are still academic institutions where appraisal has not been implemented for library staff, particularly at support staff level. In some cases this has been the result of union distrust of management's motives. It is perhaps unlikely that those institutions which have failed to implement appraisal across all grades are the kind to have a well-structured staff development programme in place. (A fuller discussion follows in the next chapter.)

Opportunities for CPD

Attempts have been made by various bodies to quantify ideal amounts of development, either by specifying a minimum number of hours per year or a minimum expenditure per head. For example, the Fielden Report[10] recommends that a minimum of 5% of staff time should be allocated to training and development. However, if CPD is truly integrated into working life, it is virtually impossible to count the amount of time spent on development. Opportunities for learning can crop up unexpectedly so everyone needs to be prepared to take full advantage of new experiences and to learn from others, even in informal situations. One of the strengths of the LA *Framework* for CPD is its recommendation that people should be encouraged to think about development in the broadest possible terms. Therefore opportunities for professional development can be found in:

- learning from the example of others
- professional reading
- coaching or mentoring
- job exchanges or shadowing
- attending courses or conferences
- participating in different activities
- open learning
- distance learning
- training others
- attending meetings.

Short courses

It remains true that a significant amount of CPD involves participating in short courses. Organizations such as the LA, ASLIB and TFPL offer a wide range of courses that meet most of the development needs of the profession. Courses appropriate to the needs of support staff are less in evidence although skills in customer service, basic IT, and effective communication are surely essential for all support staff.

Short courses may be seen as the easy option but the benefits must be maximized in order to justify the not inconsiderable costs that can be incurred. Careful preparation, evaluation and continuing practice are essential in order to make the most of the experience. As indicated earlier, course attendance should be the result of a systematic development needs analysis. Before attending, participants should be quite clear about the aims of the course and their expectations of it as well as discussing the expected outcomes with their line managers. After the course, managers should request structured feedback and agree how the newly-acquired skills or knowledge might best be put to practical use. It is fairly common for staff attending courses to have to write up a report afterwards. There is little to be gained from this practice if the report is simply filed away and the training promptly forgotten. Instead of channelling effort into writing a report it is preferable to concentrate on the pre-course preparation and the application of new skills and knowledge after the course. Such an approach enables staff development officers or managers to justify expenditure by clarifying the links between development and performance.

Professional qualifications

The value of higher education has been stressed by Judith Elkin[11] who believes that it 'allows students to develop their ability to learn and amass knowledge, to demonstrate their intellectual skills and ability to grasp new events quickly and to respond creatively and effectively'. Access to higher education is now within the reach of a far greater number and diversity of students than ever before. Within the library and information profession, distance learning and part-time courses now mean that professional qualifications can be gained by staff during the course of their employment in libraries – for instance, the distance-learning degree in Information and Library Studies currently being offered by the University of Wales, Aberystwyth. The nature of the course and its modular format mean that students have considerable flexibility over the length and content of their degree studies. Part-time, post-graduate courses, such as the MSc in Information and Library Management at Bristol University, are particularly suitable for graduates who wish to make a career in library and information work.

There is a danger that staff who are motivated to study in this way will develop unrealistic expectations of promotion or want to put their developing knowledge to practical use in the workplace. Unless properly managed, this can lead to frustration on the part of the individual who naturally wants to put new skills into practice. Equally, it can lead to the resentment of colleagues if they see one of their number seemingly being given all the most interesting work to do. Managers must also avoid the temptation to exploit these highly motivated and able staff. Naturally, support and encouragement must be given, but so must clear guidelines about the extent to which a course of study can be allowed to impinge on day-to-day work.

Conclusion

It is axiomatic that university and college libraries are engaged in the business of learning. They exist to support the learning and research needs of their parent institutions. It ought to go without saying that academic libraries have a responsibility to develop a learning culture within which library staff are supported to achieve their full potential. Of course, training is essential to make sure that everyone is equipped to perform their particular tasks and responsibilities to the highest standards. In addition, a well-managed CPD programme will encourage staff to develop their abilities beyond their immediate job needs. In a climate where development is valued and encouraged, the academic community cannot fail to benefit from services provided by library staff who are flexible, who relish a challenge and, above all, are able to respond positively to the turbulence and change that will continue to characterize the world of higher education.

References

1   Picardie, J., 'Have traditional schools had their day?', *Independent on Sunday*, 2 April 1995, 11.
2   Jones, N. and Jordan, P., *Staff management in library and information work*, 2nd edn, Aldershot, Gower, 1987, 242–3.

3   Brown, R., *A framework for continuing professional development for library and information services staff*, British Library R&D Report 6070, British Library Research and Development Department, 1992.
4   Fielden Report, 34.
5   Corrall, S., 'Staff development – whose responsibility?', *Library manager*, **9**, 1995, 10–11.
6   Noon, P., 'CPD: Professional Development – continuing and compulsory?', *Librarian career development*, **2** (4), 1994, 4–8.
7   Fisher, B., 'Professional organizations and professional development', *British journal of academic librarianship*, **9** (3), 1994, 167–78.
8   Dakers, H., 'NVQs, Follett and Fielden', *British journal of academic librarianship*, **9** (3), 1994, 179–90.
9   Wilson, T. D., 'Are NVQs for robots?', *Library Association record*, **97** (7), 1995, 381.
10   Fielden Report, 7.
11   Elkin, J., 'Higher-level NVQs: cause for concern?', *Librarian career development*, **2** (4), 1994, 32–3.

3

Appraisal and Staff Development

ROBERT OLDROYD

Introduction

This chapter examines the role of appraisal in the management of training and staff development. It considers the purpose of appraisal, the benefits both to the organization and the individual, and the means to make it successful. It is seen as having an important part to play in the wider context of human resource planning, organizational strategy and resource procurement, as well as in the development of individuals. It has been found to be a particularly helpful tool in a research-led university (Nottingham) in which library staff have to develop skills to a high level in support of services meeting the competing needs and demands of both teaching, learning and research.

Forms of appraisal

Staff appraisal may come in a variety of forms. Carole Fisher[1] has identified them as performance review, potential review and reward review. All three involve objective setting, and the use of 'stick and carrot' as motivators in varying proportions. Most university appraisal schemes focus primarily on performance and potential. Schemes generally involve an interview in which performance against the previous year's objectives is discussed, together with objective setting for the next year, all within the context of university and departmental strategic plans. Some appraisal schemes, such as that used by the Civil Service (including the British Library) are formal and heavily-documented, focusing very firmly on performance and reward. Most schemes are 'top-down', with senior or line managers as appraisers, but some favour appraisal by peers and at least one university uses 'bottom-up' appraisal for heads of department. Another, perhaps rather daunting method, involves 360 degree feedback, in which all the stakeholders in a person's performance comment on and assess that person's performance.

The aims of appraisal need to be clear, and they do vary from scheme to scheme. The 1987 CVCP/AUT document,[2] which provided a model for old university schemes for academic and related staff, stated that the aims of appraisal were to develop careers, improve performance, identify potential for promotion, and improve institutional efficiency. Some schemes for clerical staff have placed the emphasis more on benefit to the institution than the individual – improving effectiveness, providing feedback on performance, identifying people's strengths and weaknesses and having a better understanding of people's potential and, in one instance I have seen, providing managers with a formal opportunity to meet and talk with their staff!

Who is appraisal for? There is no single answer to this question in universities. A 1994 survey by SCONUL[3] indicated that 86 of 96 responding universities and colleges of higher education had appraisal schemes, and library staff were included in 83 of them. However, only in 38 instances did the scheme apply to all library staff. In 34 institutions the scheme could be modified for library-specific purposes. The missing statistic is: in how many instances were there *separate* schemes for 'professional' and 'support' staff? Some institutions certainly had different schemes for 'non-teaching' staff, and some specifically for technicians.

Should all staff necessarily use the same scheme? It is sometimes argued that different people need different kinds of appraisal, and that therefore it is inappropriate to give all staff a form which includes questions and issues which do not apply to them. There may also be a different emphasis in the expected outcomes of appraisal for different types of staff, as in the separate schemes mentioned above. At Nottingham there was much debate about whether professional library staff should use the academics' appraisal form or that for computing and administrative staff. As the latter made no provision for individuals to comment on involvement with their professional body, research activity, or publication, the form used by academics was chosen.

Is appraisal appropriate for all staff? What purpose does it serve for people who seem to have no prospects of career advancement or promotion? Does it represent time well-spent when it includes training, preparation, interviewing and dealing with outcomes, or could the time be better used?

The question is not an easy one to answer. We expect all staff to be committed to the common purpose of the organization, so we must find ways of showing that all are valued, that their needs are taken seriously, and that they all have at least the opportunity to put themselves in a position to advance their careers or become better paid. Experience demonstrates that many support staff who lack professional qualifications are keen to find ways to gain experience, and be able to justify seeking promotion. Many of them are truly committed to the organization, in ways sometimes totally disproportionate to the level of payment they receive. In short, they want as many as they can get of the advantages (as they see them) which senior staff have. This certainly applies to training in general, and particularly in electronic information systems, where many support staff show an aptitude, even a gift, not necessarily evident in all senior colleagues. And it applies to appraisal as well. For these people appraisal is definitely worthwhile, both for them and for the organization. In a way it is ironic that the question should be asked (as it frequently is) about support staff, since the well-known maxim applies as much to libraries as to any other organization – the lowest paid people are generally the most vital in keeping the service going. The quality of their performance frequently reflects the image users have of the library as a whole.

Benefits of appraisal

The organization

Realistically, there must be benefit in appraisal both to the organization and to individuals. So what are the benefits to the organization? The task of the Librarian is formidable in the face of severely limited resources with which to meet customers' ever-increasing demands and needs that change and develop with alarming speed. There is a constant need to be looking at priorities and tasks, whether they are still relevant, what new skills are needed, and whether existing staff can learn them and take on new roles. The Librarian has to be able to demonstrate to the institution that it is receiving value for money from an economic, efficient and effective service. Appraisal is a valuable tool in ensuring that staff are focusing their efforts on real needs, and on maintaining high quality. If they are not, it enables remedial action to be agreed and taken, and for any appropriate training to be authorized. It also provides a formal opportunity to link discussion of individual performance with individual and organizational objectives. In turn it contributes to identifying overall needs, and thus to the management of training and staff development. On a broader front, appraisal provides a way into the library's planning of human resources, which in turn links with strategic planning (within the university's plans) and the procurement of financial resources. At the same time it can reinforce the library's identification with the rest of the university, since many needs (particularly for transferable or IT skills training) will have been identified in other departments too. It also provides a confidential forum in which ideas for future deployment and/or promotion can be discussed. When needs change so quickly it is invaluable to have this kind of 'data resource' to hand.

The individual

From an individual's point of view, appraisal has a number of benefits. At the preparation stage it provides an opportunity for reflection and self-assessment, and to consider areas of concern which can be clarified by the appraiser. It provides a focus for all the various pressures to assess and evaluate one's own performance, whether from the institution (which in turn is pressed by its funding council), or from the Library Association which requires chartered librarians to take responsibility for their career-long continuing development. Indeed, its *Framework for continuing professional development*[4] can be very helpful in preparing for appraisal, particularly in looking at career development or job-enhancement. The appraisal interview is an opportunity to find out the line-manager's views on one's performance, to clarify one's position in the organization and to establish development needs. Clarity of roles, responsibilities and reporting lines tends to encourage good motivation and morale.

Appraisal and the management of staff development

In order for appraisal to be successful, a number of features must be evident, involving action by both library and employee. Senior managers (starting with the Librarian) must express their full commitment to and support for appraisal, and allow sufficient time and resources to enable it to take place. The library must be prepared to deliver the agreed training and development outcomes, over an agreed time-scale, with an appropriate budget allocation. An organization which does not show this commitment cannot expect its employees to demonstrate commitment either. Librarians generally accept that they are responsible for their own development, but they need the library's management to endorse that, to encourage them and to empower them to succeed. Individuals for their part must prepare thoroughly for the appraisal interview, and take the actions agreed at it.

It is a pity that at Nottingham there is as yet no official appraisal scheme for staff other than academic-related, though one is promised 'soon'. This in no way demonstrates a lack of commitment on the library's part to developing support staff or providing appropriate training opportunities for them. Sometimes one is obliged to follow institutional practice and wait for a scheme to be put in place for all support staff in the university. We do what we can in the meantime. Appraisal of academic-related staff has proved its worth many times over.

In 1993 there was a major restructuring of the library staff, in which many people's long-standing responsibilities were changed. For some this was a painful process, and for all a time of some uncertainty. The appraisal scheme for academic-related staff was well-established, and proved a valuable format within which to round off and honour past achievements, and to clarify future roles and the training required to fulfil them. Appraisal enabled librarians to discuss the future with confidence with their teams, and in turn to establish their training needs. The clear communications resulting from these processes were most helpful in smoothing the transitional path from old to new structure, and ensuring that it had the best possible chance of success. In short, appraisal proved a valuable support to the management of change.

Appraisal is helping to identify training needs relating to teaching, research and management skills. In particular, the library has developed Internet training for postgraduate students and academic staff which requires a combination of teaching skills and the knowledge of Internet sources of information relevant to Nottingham's research interests. Staff have had to develop training and presentation skills in order to deliver these popular sessions. At the same time, many 'career-grade' staff have taken on management roles for the first time, particularly since restructuring, and their needs required careful identification and programme delivery by high-quality trainers.

Appraisal schemes are not without their problems. Different organizations are at different stages of understanding the process, and they vary considerably in the degree of commitment which they demonstrate towards it. Even after several years some university librarians still see appraisal as a tedious annual chore, to be despatched as speedily as possible. When schemes affecting academic-related staff were negotiated in the late 1980s, there was considerable uncertainty and mistrust about the purpose of appraisal. In some instances the tone of the scheme changed dramatically between the first draft and the final version – from a method of weeding out under-achievers to one which encouraged and supported people to optimize their skills, and to improve their performance. Anything which linked appraisal with promotion or financial reward was negotiated out, a move which perhaps helped to accelerate the introduction of performance-related pay in universities.

Another issue was (and remains) confidentiality. Who precisely should have access to appraisal documentation? As a result of mistrust in some universities, schemes were negotiated which confined any knowledge of the outcome of appraisal and its documentation to the appraisee, appraiser and head of department. The result was that although training and staff development actions were agreed, training officers were not allowed to know about them, so could neither budget for nor deliver them. At least one institution allowed the head of department to tell the training officer that particular training was needed, but not by whom! The reluctance of any member of staff to lay bare his or her training needs (or weaknesses as some would view them) is understandable, but there needs to be the freedom for such information to be used, albeit with care and sensitivity, or appraisal is a meaningless exercise – like a piece of research whose results are not allowed to be known. While it is inappropriate for appraisal documents to be widely circulated, it is essential that those responsible for training have a full picture of their staff's training and development needs (*including* those which emerge from appraisal) so that they can plan to meet them. There is no reason why an appraisal document cannot have a separate sheet on which the appraisee's training or development needs are listed, and which can be used with discretion by a training officer.

A related issue is trust. Even if senior management are fully-committed to it, the chosen scheme must be seen to be transparently workable, and both appraisers and appraisees must have confidence in it. In addition, appraisees must trust their appraiser to the extent of feeling able to say anything at all without it being used in some other context. This is perhaps easier in organizations where a general climate of trust and openness exists. In others it is impossible, and the quality of appraisal outcomes suffer as a result. Serious questions should be asked in the latter cases about the management style of the library.

An often-voiced criticism of appraisal is that it takes up a great deal of time. Aside from considerations about regarding staff as the greatest asset or greatest liability, the fact is that appraisal does absorb much time for all concerned. All the more reason then that the time should be well-spent! Proper training of both appraisers and appraisees is essential. Though bodies like the Industrial Society recommend (and indeed carry out) at least two days' training for each group, it is well-known that many institutions skimp it. Some schemes require large quantities of time for preparation. This is understandable for some appraisees, but three hours' preparation by an appraiser for one interview in a scheme I have seen recently seems excessive.

One thing which appraisal does not and cannot do is to elicit an organizational or managerial perspective on who needs what training and staff development, and the relative priority of achieving individual or library ambitions. While appraisers should not be agreeing actions which they know cannot be delivered, they will not always have a full picture and so may agree them in good faith, ignorant of other higher priorities. Within the overall context of the library's plans there will be certain training needs which are of the highest priority, and which may affect large numbers of staff, some of them significantly. Where there is conflict, or a particularly tight budget, the library's managerial priorities are almost bound to take precedence. Where this occurs, it needs to be clearly understood by appraisers, who must make allowance at the next appraisal for the non-achievement of some agreed objectives by individuals.

Appraisal is not intended to be a substitute for a full training needs analysis. When attempts are made to establish needs, a number of methods may be used, each contributing to the whole. Appraisal is one, matching individuals' objectives with those of the library or service. Another is the training interview, used successfully at Nottingham University with library assistants. This is an annual discussion between assistants and supervisors to focus specifically on training needs, whether task-related or broader transferable skills. It is an occasion when managers or supervisors voice their perceptions of their teams, and individuals within it consider their own perceptions of themselves. As staff have become familiar with the process (new staff are trained as part of induction) needs are now identified by individuals updating their training records annually.

One worrying feature, surprisingly common even after some years of appraisal schemes, is that some university chief librarians still take an ad hoc approach to training and staff development, allowing only those who ask for it to go to a conference or training event, take no steps to encourage all staff or at least those identified as needing it, have no policy, and do not budget properly for it. They continue to see training solely in terms of going out of the institution on courses, which are therefore perceived as expensive and likely to yield little benefit – surely not their own experience. What real value or meaning can appraisal have in those institutions? At Nottingham there is a requirement for heads of department to report annually on the process of appraisal, and to list training and development needs which might be met by the University Staff Training and Development Unit. This monitoring, plus a clear (never yet used) appeals procedure, ensures that appraisal is taken seriously and carried out to a satisfactory standard.

Conclusion

To summarize, if appraisal is used constructively and positively it is a valuable tool in establishing training and staff development needs, and in ensuring that they are taken seriously and delivered. It can benefit the library in relation to all types of staff (despite the time it takes) though one common scheme may not always be suitable for everybody. Appraisal makes a valuable contribution to library strategic planning, especially human resource planning. However, maximum value will only be obtained if both management and staff are committed to it. Procedural problems are easily solved provided that all have confidence in the scheme and are assured that information will not be misused. The biggest contribution which appraisal can make to the library's development is in the management of change, since it provides a formal yet 'user-friendly' environment in which difficult issues can be aired, and positive outcomes guaranteed.

References

1   Fisher, C., *Staff appraisal*, Solihull College of Technology, 1993.
2   Committee of Vice-Chancellors and Principals and Association of University Teachers, *Career development and staff appraisal procedures for academic and academic-related staff*, London, CVCP, 1987.
3   Standing Conference of National and University Libraries, *Sconul library profiles 1993–94*, London, SCONUL, 1995.
4   The Library Association, *The framework for continuing professional development: your personal profile*, London, The Library Association, 1992. (Issued free to members).

4

The Quality Framework

MAXINE MELLING

Introduction

This chapter reviews the quality programmes and initiatives which impact increasingly on academic libraries and considers their importance to the strategic management of staff development and training.

A number of common themes pervade current professional concerns with both quality and human resource management. In particular, both stress that effective and efficient organizations are those which recognize the central role played by staff. These organizations use management strategies to enable employees to take a more active role than before, whilst ensuring that they have the skills and abilities to accept this role. This theme of employee involvement and responsibility should be central to any consideration of the quality framework.

Quality movement

Introduction

The background and development of the current quality movement has been documented and reviewed by a number of excellent critics and exponents. It is not the purpose of this chapter to rehearse these arguments. However, a brief resume of the main systems is necessary to an understanding of their impact on human resource management.

Quality assurance

The current quality assurance movement has its roots in the period during and immediately following the Second World War.

Documented standards were developed at this time to help control the quality of the production process of high-value, complex weapons systems. Although the quality assurance movement has developed considerably in the intervening years, it is still associated with the production process and with terminology which is often more readily associated with the production of so-many widgets than with, for example, the education of students. This comment is not intended as adverse criticism of quality assurance systems but is made in order to highlight the cultural difficulties faced by service organizations which may choose this route to quality and the need to address attitudinal as well as skills-based training.

As a result of its history, quality assurance is often associated with aspects of quality control such as end-inspection and the return of faulty goods. However, quality assurance is actually concerned with removing the need for end-inspection by preventing error. Quality assurance systems aim to achieve this end by meeting specified levels of service and thereby removing the root cause of poor quality. Quality assurance systems are therefore based on the clear documentation of processes, as well as regular audit and evaluation, to ensure consistency of practice and continuous improvement.

A core principle of quality assurance, and one which runs throughout the quality movement, is that quality is everyone's responsibility. In consequence, all staff should be involved in the development of a quality assurance system through, for example, the writing of procedures and work instructions and active participation as internal auditors of the system. Training programmes will inevitably vary depending on local circumstances, but these core principles require organization-wide awareness training in the system itself. In addition, as quality-related staff responsibilities are identified and as processes and the core-competences linked to them are documented, the requirement for skills-based training will also become evident.

Quality audit and assessment have become a familiar aspect of further and higher education in recent years. The quality assurance systems which are operated within colleges and universities are monitored by the funding and quality councils and are the subject of both institutional quality audit and subject-based assessment. Library and learning resource provision, always an important part of this type of assessment, has been brought into very close focus by the inclusion of learning resources as a core aspect of the Higher Education Funding Council's subject assessments. These core aspects are graded and determine a subject's overall rating. As this type of audit of learning resource provision becomes widespread, academic librarians need sophisticated management information and the managerial abilities to use it. The Follett Report emphasized the importance of establishing a coherent and generic set of performance indicators (PIs) as soon as possible. This recommendation reflects an increasing awareness of the accountability of academic libraries and the need to play a proactive role in quality assurance procedures within the sector.

The greater focus placed on accountability has been highlighted by Sheila Corrall[1] in her analysis of the Fielden Report and the management development needs of academic librarians. Corrall argues that academic libraries in the United Kingdom have a poor history of management development in comparison with the United States and advises that the increasing importance placed on accountability and quality requires a greater emphasis on this level of staff development and training. Corrall suggests a number of core skills which should be included in a management development programme. However, she also makes the point that management development is 'as much about encouraging a managerial ethos throughout the organisation as it is about developing specific skills'.

This point mirrors the importance placed by the quality movement on developing a quality culture, rather than attempting to graft specific aspects of quality systems onto the existing culture. Awareness training and the development of creative and analytical skills are therefore of equal, if not more importance, than skills-based training.

Total Quality Management

Nigel Butterwick[2] defines Total Quality Management (TQM) as

the approach which organizations adopt to improve their performance on a systematic and continuous basis . . . achieved via the involvement of employees throughout the organization in satisfying the total requirements of every customer . . . and the development of processes within the organization which are error-free.

This definition illustrates that systems such as quality assurance can, and often are, used as part of a TQM approach. TQM itself, however, can be defined as much more than a quality system and, rather, as a set of beliefs and behaviours which comprise an organizational culture. TQM combines the use of detailed process control and error-free production standards, using such systems as published standards, problem-solving techniques and statistical analysis, with a commitment to attitudinal change. The latter shifts emphasis onto the identification of customer requirements, for both internal and external customers, and places great importance on enabling and involving all employees, moving control from outside the individual to within. An organization adopting a TQM approach must be committed to continuous improvement, where the norm is operating right first-time. As with other quality systems, TQM requires full commitment from senior management and a top-down approach to the development of quality. All staff in an organization committed to TQM are therefore affected by and involved in the organization's commitment to quality.

A core principle of TQM is the importance of identifying and meeting customer requirements. The system proposes a very particular definition of the customer, emphasizing that he or she should not be defined simply in terms of the end user, i.e. the external customer, but that colleagues should also be included in the definition, i.e. the internal customer. TQM advocates the recognition of a customer-supplier chain with the need to agree requirements throughout an organization and to recognize the chain-link interdependency of people and departments.

The emphasis placed on the customer by TQM is very important to the changes taking place in libraries, as traditional organizational structures are re-assessed in light of the need to deal effectively with rapid change. Hazel Dakers,[3] in discussing the need for National Vocational Qualifications (NVQs) in the library and information community, points to an enforced 'delayering' in libraries, with decision making taking place at a level much closer to the customer. TQM's requirement for all staff to identify their immediate customers and to clarify customer requirements links closely to this development. The staff training and development needs associated with these changes are considerable. Dakers makes an explicit link between NVQs and the quality movement, pointing to the emphasis placed by NVQs on generic, transferable standards which allow staff to develop skills associated with customer care.

TQM purports to engender significant cultural change, to involve large numbers of employees in teamwork and the use of problem-solving techniques and to require rigorous process control. It is hardly surprising, therefore, that emphasis is also placed on the need to develop a quality training policy. Such a policy should incorporate the allocation of training responsibilities and the definition of training objectives.

The recommendation to develop a training policy, linked closely to the organizational mission and goals, is not exclusive to TQM. 'Investors In People' (IIP) also stresses the importance of a corporate approach and responsibility for staff development and training and emphasizes the need to set individual aims and objectives clearly within this framework. This aspect of quality management is also reflected in the recommendations of the Fielden Report, which stress the importance of developing staff training policies which identify responsibility for training and link training plans to institutional planning.

Paul Spenley[4] has developed a training model for TQM which illustrates the types of training recommended for staff throughout an organization. In this model he identifies four different levels of training, including the top management team, middle management, first line supervisors and operational staff. Spenley argues that all staff should receive training in the principles of total quality and in problem solving techniques. First line supervisors and above should also receive training in team leadership, whilst middle and senior managers should receive additional training in business strategy and performance measures. The central tenet of Spenley's argument is that all staff should know what is required of TQM and be able to use the basic tools to solve problems at their level of operation. He stresses that training should operate on a cascade principle, with managers training their own staff in order to demonstrate their own commitment to quality. Any organization adopting a TQM approach must address the costs of this level of commitment. Spenley justifies the commitment required by pointing out that the cost of non-conformance is rarely measured and may typically be up to 40% of turnover in western service industries.

Training for quality

Introduction

Barrie Dale[5] has argued that:

> A planned programme of training and education in quality-related skills for
> *all* employees . . . is an essential prerequisite for successful and permanent
> quality improvement.

The relatively brief overview of the quality framework given above
has hopefully highlighted the range of training and development
issues that need to be considered within such a programme. These
issues are explored in further detail below. Of course, many library
managers are addressing such concerns without explicit reference to
formal quality systems. To claim that the identification of customer
requirements or the development of team building skills, for example, is unique to the quality movement would be absurd. In addition,
many of the issues highlighted by the Fielden Report, such as the
development of customer service initiatives, the increase in team
working and the empowerment of library assistants, are closely associated with the current quality movement. However, the context of
quality audit and accountability within which academic libraries
now operate and the growth in influence of systems such as TQM
have highlighted a range of complementary skills which can be identified as being of direct relevance to the current quality framework.

Cultural change

Introducing a quality-oriented approach to the ways in which people
work calls for changes in behaviour and in working procedures. The
effects of this type of change, on all levels of staff, should not be
underestimated and cannot be considered without first providing
organization-wide awareness training. This training should address
issues such as the organization's quality policy, including its definition of quality and how responsibilities for quality have been allocated. It is also important that staff share a common vocabulary and
do not feel either alienated or suspicious of new terminology and
working practices.

Different groups of staff may require different types of training in
relation to quality. However, it is imperative that all staff are included
in awareness training. The cross-departmental boundaries in organi-

zations can be one of the weakest points in relation to quality improvement. This weakness is exaggerated if one, or both, of the functions involved lack the relevant awareness and understanding of the organization's quality programme.

One of the key aspects of quality management is the responsibility placed on staff for ensuring that a quality service is achieved and the empowerment of all staff in order to achieve this end. This can represent a considerable challenge both to managers' feelings of status and security and to staff who may not want to be empowered! Lack of commitment from either group almost inevitably leads to the failure of any quality initiative. An interesting example of this can be found in the quality circles movement which flourished briefly during the 1980s. Of all the quality circles started in the UK during this period, 90% had been discontinued by the end of the decade. There are obviously a range of explanations for this failure. However, a common theme would appear to be the use of quality circles as an add-on to existing cultures without first ensuring management commitment. Research into the quality circles movement[6] has indicated that middle managers believed this type of staff participation to offer small returns for high levels of disruption to the existing lines of power and communication. Managers refused to accept the work carried out by staff in the circles, resulting in a reduction in participation and eventual failure.

Management skills

The threat posed to senior and middle managers by organizational change has been highlighted in the Fielden Report. The Report emphasizes that new forms of operation, such as team working, will be necessary to achieve effective change in libraries and highlights the need to provide training support for managers threatened by these developments.

Barrie Dale[7] has identified an emphasis by managers in the UK on what he calls 'transactional' leadership. This type of leadership is associated with crisis management, and is characterized by reactive rather than proactive behaviour. Dale argues that managers committed to quality should practise 'transforming' leadership. Typically, 'transforming' managers plan strategically for organizational change. In identifying quality management skills, Dale highlights the ability to communicate, to sell ideas, to teach and to manage projects. The importance placed on communication is illustrative of the TQM principle of cascaded training, where senior managers learn the tools and techniques associated with TQM and then pass them on to other staff.

Quality management makes considerable demands upon managers, both to learn and communicate new skills and techniques and to accommodate what may be dramatic attitudinal and cultural changes. Appropriate and effective training and development of senior and middle managers is therefore crucial to libraries operating within a quality framework.

Training for empowerment

Quality systems incorporate a range of methods by which staff are empowered to make changes and contribute directly to the improvement of quality. These methods include the development of team work, the use of problem-solving techniques, job rotation, the use of quality circles and the delegation of authority for decision making about customer service issues. In addition to the need to address these skills, the adoption of a quality management approach may also highlight the need for basic job-related skills training. One aspect of the quality management approach is the identification of core competences and the specification of work procedures. Inevitably, this may highlight skills short-falls that have not previously been identified and which must be addressed.

The emphasis placed by quality systems on problem-solving and on the sharing of ideas leads, inevitably, to the use of team work and collaboration. In order for teams to work effectively staff must be kept informed of the 'big picture' and be given a clear understanding of how their jobs, and the contribution of their team to the organization, fit into the planning cycle. The types of skills required for effective team work typically include interactive and consensus building skills, problem solving and communication skills, using techniques such as Pareto Analysis (or the 80/20 rule), cause and effect analysis and brainstorming. (Interested readers may wish to consult the increasing literature on quality and will find excellent descriptions of the relevant tools and techniques in both Oakland and Bank.[8, 9])

Quality systems such as ISO 9000 and IIP make explicit the need to identify core competences and for the need to link these to the use of professional development plans for staff which are reviewed on a regular basis. The stated aims of the IIP initiative are to ensure that training and development are planned, related to business goals, driven by standards and evaluated. The very practical approach of these systems is also exemplified by the NVQ movement which places emphasis on the assessment of people, preferably in the workplace, for what they can do, rather than for what they know. This concentration on work-based skills which are directly linked to work-based concerns has its dangers. One of the main criticisms of the NVQ movement is that it is inward looking, concentrating on what people can already do, rather than ensuring further development. However, the clear identification of the skills needed to carry out a specific task does ensure that relevant training is provided and that staff feel not only *empowered* but also *enabled* to participate. If staff are to be persuaded to take greater responsibility for quality and to participate in team work they must be helped to develop the requisite technical and personal skills.

John Oakland,[10] one of the British gurus of quality management, has stated that training is 'the single most important factor in actually improving quality'. In order to ensure that the training function is given this central role, it is imperative that the quality policy provides a framework within which training activities are planned and operated, that responsibility for training is made explicit and lies with line management, and that training objectives are clearly defined. In addition, records of the training carried out by staff and the extent to which training has met stated objectives must be maintained. Systems such as ISO 9000, NVQs and IIP all contain references to the control of training records through either the development of core competency records or records of achievement.

Conclusion

The quality framework described in this chapter is one of accountability, audit and rapid change. Its concerns are with the central role played by staff in the delivery of a quality service and the need to ensure that all staff in an organization are provided with the skills and understanding to accept this role. In addition, the requirement for continuous improvement makes it essential that skills are updated as services change to meet changing customer needs.

The quality programmes and initiatives outlined above offer a strategic approach for managers to deliver training which meets the requirements for quality. This approach provides a framework for staff training through the development of training policies which are linked to organizational aims and objectives and which are the responsibility of line management. Professional development programmes and the identification of the skills needed to carry out specified duties help to place the individual's role within the broader organizational context, whilst awareness and skills-based training provide staff with the ability to accept responsibility for quality.

Many of the issues discussed here as part of the quality framework are also addressed in the Fielden Report. Indeed, a number of Fielden's recommendations, such as the development of a training policy and the nomination of a senior member of staff with formal responsibility for training, can be identified within the strategic approach described above. The convergence of current library concerns and the core principles of many quality initiatives is indicative of the impact of the quality framework on academic libraries and the importance placed by them on the continued delivery of quality services within a context of rapid change. Most importantly, it highlights a growing awareness of the key role played by all library staff in delivering quality services and the need to develop training and development strategies which facilitate it.

References

1   Corrall, S., 'Management development in academic libraries', *British journal of academic librarianship*, **9** (3), 1994, 209-23.
2   Butterwick, N., 'Total quality management in the University Library', *Library management*, **14** (3), 1993, 28–31.
3   Dakers, H., 'NVQs, Follett and Fielden', *British journal of academic librarianship*, **9** (3), 1994, 179–90.
4   Spenley, P., *World class performance through total quality: a practical guide to implementation*, London, Chapman and Hall, 1992, 93.
5   Lascelles, D. M. and Dale, B. G., 'Difficulties and barriers to quality improvement'. In Dale, B., *Managing quality*, 2nd. edn, London, Prentice Hall, 1994, 325.
6   Hill, S., 'Why quality circles failed but total quality management might succeed', *British journal of industrial relations*, **29** (4), 1991, 541–68.
7   *Ibid.*, 320.

8 Oakland, J. S., *Total quality management: the route to improving performance*, 2nd. edn, Oxford, Butterworth Heinemann, 1993.

9 Bank, J., *The essence of total quality management*, Prentice Hall, 1992.

10 *Ibid.*, 387.

5

The Learning Framework

NIK POLLARD

Introduction

We seek to develop our members of staff by improving their ability to analyse and perform tasks and to deal with other people. This mutually beneficial process needs to be carefully and sensitively managed against desired outcomes i.e. against the agreed purpose and role of the library service within the home institution and its wider aims. For most academic libraries in the United Kingdom, their essential function continues to be the support of teaching and research, with 'teaching' support the primary function. However, those widespread social changes and pressures which have moved us away from a consensus view that the socially and personally appropriate model is staff training, towards one centred on the continuous development of the individual within work and project teams, have produced parallel changes in the practices and underlying models of teaching. This has in itself changed the nature of the desired outcomes towards which we aim and produced present or predictable emphases for the role of information workers and their development needs. This chapter will examine the nature of these changes, how they have come about, the effect on how students learn and staff teach, the changing role of librarians and other information workers in the new models and practices of learning delivery and the concomitant needs for staff development. This chapter is written from the viewpoint of a long-term librarian of one of the new universities.

The context of change

A wide range of factors makes the end of the twentieth century a period of accelerating change which has produced some marked and inter-related effects. The complexity of technology and the fierceness of economic competition have effectively disenfranchized large numbers, either excluding them from the charmed circles of employment, knowledge and quality of life or causing them to suffer as their economic and cultural group falls behind. At the same time, global communications media have created a commonality of basic social awareness and aspiration, wider than those groups fully in ownership of the ways of life represented. Their pervasive availability has also contributed to a breakdown in the consensus support for traditional social structures and life patterns. A major emphasis in this common culture is upon individuality and choice/consumerism.

They have, on the one hand, created a new form of literacy combining, and possibly transcending, both print and image even while the separate formats continue to have specific strengths for particular communications purposes, while on the other, creating a new structure of knowledge, allowing a clearer daily separation between understanding and information and its availability. These factors have inevitably affected work and education. Nations need a sophisticated work force in order to compete in the global industrial/commercial environment. Those governments that subsidized one-off degree level education are finding it difficult to continue with this in the face of world-wide competition, population numbers, individual demand and the requirement for lifelong education. Many have moved in the direction of more effective institutions (to reduce cost and increase throughput) as well as self-funded students. At the same time they must increase the age participation rate and continuous education in order to stay competitive and avoid social disruption.

Employers faced with fierce competition and moving markets need flexible, self starting employees capable of embracing change, good at acquiring and using knowledge and happy to work individually or in teams.

Individuals need continuous education in order to match a moving employment market and are encouraged by their social/economic aspirations. In selecting education they increasingly require the choice and personal appropriateness available to them in the commercial environment and modelled for them in the communications media.

Traditional structures of educational delivery, especially in Western Europe, reflect the demands of a seventeenth century agrarian economy and culture where a small, élitist group, taught transfer of knowledge from the knowledgeable master to the ignorant pupil, in a seasonal pattern which allows for summer release to help with the harvest. Under pressure from numbers, reducing funding levels, resource shortages and genuine demand for appropriate and timely learning throughout life, these models are ever less viable useful or marketable.

Similarly, the underlying models of the learning process have tended to reflect a passing world in which the acquired wisdom of one generation was generally usable for, or readable by, the next; in which the principle corpus of knowledge, largely theoretical and philosophical, was expensive to record and possess and which was practically and economically transferable through the medium of the wise teacher and role learning. This world view both permitted and required the formal, one-off education of a limited elite (first social, latterly professional and usually male) who were seen to be the natural heirs to the objective world of recorded knowledge and explanation, while the bulk of the population was restricted to a limited formal education. Equally, it limited educability/learning to the period of physical maturation. This model, too, has become less viable and appropriate. Technical change and the educative efforts of global media have been particularly significant influences. They have broken the chain of received wisdom, permitting people to demonstrate that skill and ability are not exclusive to age, caste or authority, and have created a world of changing employment which excludes the unskilled and forces the active and employed to refine their skills continually .

Educational institutions are faced with difficult decisions as to the rate at which it is sensible to embed new means of communication into the curriculum or to shape new kinds of delivery around them. 'Sensible' here covers issues of content (relevance and depth), connectivity, affordability, competitiveness (between educational deliverers and market availability), readability i.e. framed sufficiently within the cultural mainstream to ensure relevance and accessibility.

New models of learning

New models of effective learning have emerged which reflect this environment and stress:

- deep understanding as against surface or rote learning
- skills against knowledge
- a related differentiation between analytic/synthetic, interpersonal and practical skills
- that people learn differently from each other, through each other and in different ways at different times in their live.
- the reinforcing effects of learning by doing in its widest sense
- group interaction as against individual competition
- the helpful effects of a designed balance between learning, interaction with peer learners and the tutor, reinforcement and benign neglect
- the centrality of the learner and his/her skills, together with the need for them to possess the process for themselves. (It is worth reflecting here on the difference between student-centred and independent learning.)

The pervasive information environment and its different media and search tools are crucial to the appropriateness and applicability of these new models since they permit a much clearer practical differentiation between understanding (the possession of knowledge, particularly underlying principles) and the ability to use it ('skills') and knowledge (what is known, fact, data). This has clarified the emphasis on individuals and their progress, the differentiation between types of skills and the recognition that, in an information-rich environment, competent individuals can acquire knowledge and act, particularly if they have core understanding. This has forced a revaluation of notions of 'discipline' and 'corpus of knowledge' and a re-balancing against personal skills.

The interlocked combination of increasing student numbers, diversity and attendance modes, the desire/rationale for independent learning, a declining unit of resource and a need to use recorded information more at a time when prices are rising and the means of information delivery are changing rapidly has born particularly hard on the nexus between courses and resources. This has been very marked in the United Kingdom and resulted in the Follett Report and a number of sector-wide, top-slice funded initiatives.

Structures and delivery methods

Higher education systems around the world have responded with a pragmatic mixture of new structures and delivery methods. They reflect, in equal part, a genuine ideological shift towards student and learning centred models, in order to provide the more flexible offering needed by their more diverse students and employers, as well as a panic to stay economically viable and survive. A brief review of these is followed by an analysis of their implications for academic support services.

Modularity

Modularity is the restructuring of separate award routes into components which allow common sessions on particular topics to be shared between students studying cognate disciplines. It allows savings in provision but necessitates a comprehensive and well-understood organizational framework to operate effectively.

NVQs (National Vocational Qualifications) and CATs (Credit Accumulation and Transfer)

NVQs are an attempt to break down and codify the skills and competences necessary for specific discipline/professional areas, so that individual achievement can be measured. CATs are a system by which most courses and their main components carry a points award and the successful, or even partially successful, completer carries those forward between courses and/or institutions and across time as a record of personal achievement, moving up levels as points are acquired. At present, there is limited inter-changeability across the UK.

Study and information handling skills

Much detailed discipline content is now secondary to an ability to find, analyse, understand and apply information. Students need to be taught these skills.

Project work

Active learning, rather than a passive receipt of knowledge, is fundamental to the new models of learning, and project work provides a very useful blend, combining learning by explanation/doing with the exercise and improvement of skills of analysis, synthesis and exposition around a topic or discipline-related core. Project work can be used with individuals or groups, in the latter case passing on awareness of the nature of the 'work' environment and the advantages of different roles within team work, as well as improving interpersonal skills. It is a good way of introducing or reinforcing more formally delivered teaching. As a vehicle, it can be used with laboratory or field work in order to transfer practical skills, or around learning resources (print, video, computer software, data sets etc.) to transfer study skills.

Group work

Groups, especially tutorial groups, function in much the same way, except that here the emphasis is oriented more towards interpersonal and presentation skills. Again the session often centres on a particular learning resource.

Resource based learning

This is increasingly replacing or supplementing teaching. The use of learning materials takes place at a range of levels and to fulfil a variety of functions. These range from enhancing conventionally taught courses through substituting for activities which work less well with large numbers (e.g. lectures and tutorials), substituting for activities which are resource constrained (laboratory experiments, library use, field trips etc.) or facilitating student self pacing through to full blown, distance learning on and off campus.[1]

The role of the teacher

All these changes have emphasized the different but equally valid roles for academic and other staff in the design and management of learning on the one hand, and direct teaching and learner support on the other. Under traditional models, the great majority of effort, and therefore cost, goes into delivery. New models of learning are best supported by a greater investment in prior design which gives benefit on several levels.

The shape, style and method of learning delivery are selected to achieve desired learning outcomes which have to be articulated in advance. Conscious attention is given to the mix of information transfer, skills enhancement and reinforcement as well as to the possibilities of fast tracking or remedial support for those experiencing difficulties. It produces known structures more hospitable to diversity of ability and attendance modes. It does not preclude a role for the gifted teacher nor does it reduce the importance of spontaneous variation to develop themes and reinforce learning; rather, it channels and focuses these on those who most need it. It does not reduce the costs of design/delivery to present cohort sizes but, given accurate and trusted course costing mechanisms, stands to clarify decision making and allow additional student throughput at lower unit costs. It ensures learner satisfaction and limits staff and resource overload.

The greater efficacy and efficiency of many of these techniques frequently remains unproved. Their introduction results equally from the kind of heady but dubious mixture of ideological conviction and economic/political imperatives which has proved so dangerous in the past. Nonetheless, their widespread adoption seems to indicate a general consensus that they are the best and only route forward.

New roles and skills

What does all this mean for the roles of librarians and other information workers and the skills they need in order to fulfil them? In particular, it means that learning resource providers are ever more significant to the processes of course design and delivery. Along with the re-balancing and separation of course design and delivery has gone a blurring between academic activities and the work of the infrastructure units that support them, especially the academic support services (computing, library and media). On the one hand, these units control and offer the resources which are committed by the process of course design. On the other, once the course is running, they are actually delivering elements of the curriculum and this means that timely and appropriate availability are most important, especially where quality and student satisfaction are being externally monitored. In most practical senses these services are now, or should be, a part of the course team.

As a result, staff, especially professional librarians, need to know a great deal about the courses they serve and to have close formal and informal relationships with the academic units at all levels. Equally, they need to know about their institution's internal quality structure for course validation and review. However, it has to be recognized that course design, at least early on, is often very local and frequently takes place in corridors and passing conversations.

Most university libraries have adopted team structures shaped to that of the faculties and departments in order to bring them closer and give a sense of local ownership with all the dangers and advantages of librarians 'going native'. Most libraries have a degree of formal engagement with their academic committee structures. Many librarians, particularly those in the new universities, are playing a much fuller and more participative role in course design, simply because the process is having to take place earlier and in more detail. Others are getting formally engaged in the processes of validation and review with all the advantages of knowledge, exposure and contact that this brings. The same is true of involvement in external quality assessment.

A considerable difficulty is that the impact of new delivery shapes like modularity can tend to diffuse responsibility and cost centre structures can remove it to inaccessible levels. This erosion of traditionally appropriate academic structures has meant the actual or effective removal in some institutions of Boards of Study, Faculty/Departmental Boards and the Academic Board. All this makes it difficult to know who to talk to about what and, more significantly, can increase the number of relevant contact points beyond the ability to deal with them. Similarly, some institutions have begun to make validation and review more of a localized responsibility in order to ensure local ownership/responsibility. This too hides and spreads the process, making it more difficult to engage with. The development of validation and review structures as a means of systematic, cross institutional quality control has been less marked in the old universities for reasons of greater historical autonomy, past investment and more diverse present income streams. Similar comments apply to contact with research activity and awareness of the research selectivity exercise.

This requirement for liaison emphasizes the need for interpersonal skills particularly those of assertion, tact, identification, case making and negotiation. It also calls for the ability to work well in teams, to practise multi-tasking and prioritization (since effective liaison depends on and is in addition to those essential duties which keep services operational) and to think coolly, separating out loyalty to local interests (library and/or faculty) from service continuity, resource constraints and benefit to users. Equally important are a knowledge of current thinking in educational development and an ability to cost activities, given that librarians are now important to the process of change and resultant financial implications. Reliability, too, is an important issue as is an ability to detect, and use, links and levers of communication within the whole of the institutional community. Links with related service departments such as student services, property services and educational development can be critical. So too can the degree of autonomy and devolved responsibility given to professional staff. Libraries where the departmental structure necessitates such staff having to go to someone else first to give their client group decisions or answers, inevitably corrode credibility. Equally, it is important that the structures of responsibility and service provision within library departments are opaque to users.

Running alongside all this is the requirement – necessitated by complexity and resource scarcity – for there to be clear agreement about what will or will not be done, about what can or cannot be afforded. For most of us this means service agreements, service reviews and links into corporate planning and budgeting. These call for many of the skills discussed above as well as ability in analysing, estimating, planning and the clear writing of contractual type documents. One beneficial result of this careful climate of prescription and of limited budgets is that most innovation is now achieved by cooperative agreement, teamwork and project development. Project work calls for very particular skills of management, time and cost estimating, team work and supervision, reporting and frequently, technical skills.

The skills needed to assure service delivery are fairly similar and can be usefully but somewhat artificially examined from the angles of support for teachers and researchers and support for learners (no implied hierarchy!).

Skills for support of teaching

In discussing the notion of the expanded course team and the links between courses and resources, a major set of necessary skills was identified. However, there are some additional activity areas of fundamental importance which need their own particular mixes of skills. These include the following.

1. The identification of potentially relevant learning resources and passing on of details to teachers. This will include some elements of assessment such as direct and indirect costs associated with different media, availability, numbers required, user preferences and so on but generally not content assessment.
Skills: analysis, financial and interpersonal.

2. Making selected resources available within agreed constraints of numbers, time and cost. This will include ordering, payment of purchase, hire and/or licence costs. The resources must be made accessible to students and other users via cataloguing and classification, availability of read/replay devices or by computer mounting. Acquiring rights of reproduction may also be included (several university libraries offer copyright clearance and advice).
Skills: financial, organizational, technical (particularly IT), project planning and facilities management. With some new media, negotiation skills are also very significant. Legal knowledge.

3. Reporting back on such availability and costs incurred.
Skills: analytical, financial, use of IT/report writing, interpersonal and presentation.

4. Reporting back on the use made of these and other resources such as study spaces to inform judgements on the effectiveness of course designs.
Skills: statistics, collection and analysis, performance indicator construction, use of IT/report writing, interpersonal and presentation and negotiation (librarians often have to act as the spokesperson for learners).

In practice, many of these activities are carried out in close cooperation with academic and library colleagues. Nonetheless it illustrates the very wide range of skills now demanded of professional library staff and the complexity of ensuring that they receive a sufficient and balanced mix of formal training and informal learning opportunities.

Skills for support of research

Support for research requires most of these skills with the addition of conventional library skills of research and newer skills of automated selective dissemination of information (SDI) and network navigation.

Skills for support of learners

Support for learners engages all levels of library staff and demands a wide range of skills. It is here that the impact of new patterns of learning delivery are producing new forms of support requiring new kinds of supporters with new mixes of skills. It is also here that the new forms of delivery and the pressures to which they are a response have resulted in the greatest pressures and discontinuities for academic support staff. The staff development issues are examined through the principal activity areas beginning with the most traditional.

Materials availability

The arrangement, presentation and issue of physical materials are the traditional information management skills of librarians. These are being applied with equal success to electronic information sources. However, the pressure of rising learner numbers at more varied times and in more varied patterns combined with de-facto and frequently under-designed shifts from taught to independent learning have not been matched by investment. The result is an acknowledged shortage of learning materials for students, at a time when they are expected to use them more. Indeed, some of the new delivery structures have only exacerbated the problems. The elements of clustering and choice in modular schemes, especially of the 'pick and mix' variety, make for great difficulty in estimating student numbers in advance and give library systems particular problems in supplying, at short notice, groups between two and 200 all requiring the same information at the same time. Along with this has gone an increasing diversity of function at issue desks – sales of material, equipment loan and so on. The general outcome is complexity and aggression and a need to ensure that routines and processes are clear, effective and well understood by staff and users. The pressure bears particularly hard on the lowest paid, junior members of staff as frustrated learners with marketplace expectations of choice and service take it out on the nearest authority figure to hand or on each other by way of hiding and vandalism. The structure is, sadly, sometimes exacerbated by the very diversity of students now recruited.

Skills: (in addition to those traditionally associated with operations (a) user related – customer care, assertiveness, handling difficult situations, legal awareness, finance; (b) staff related – supervisory, counselling.

Facilities management

Many universities in the United Kingdom are bringing together all the learning resources needed by students in order to provide a seamless clarity of provision and to achieve operational efficiencies in doing so. The underlying model is that of the 'one-stop shop'. In the case of electronic resources this means single screens and easy navigation. In the case of physical resources this means a concentric clustering around reception/issue desks with staff mediated services adjacent and self service areas on the perimeter. Generally it includes study places with and without networked computing, quiet and group study areas including bookable rooms, self service facilities for materials editing and creation, physical learning resources and associated replay equipment, and materials issue and help desks. The very variety, scale and required availability of such facilities demand a wide range of skills, not least because some operational areas such as maintenance, renewal and cleaning are under the control of others.

Skills: new technical skills notably IT and building/environmental factors, safety and security, supervision, finance, standards setting and checking, statistics gathering and analysis, report writing and presentation and forward planning and execution.

Helping users

The emphasis on independent learning and the undoubted changes and convergences in the means of information transfer make it sensible and economic to support learners with clear and simple sources of help.

Many institutions are functionally or organizationally converging their academic support staff while recognizing distinct and important functional staff roles within a seamless service for users. One of the most significant areas of overlap is in help desk provision where it is reasonable for students to expect to get answers on computing, library and media service matters, the whereabouts of toilets and so on and the availability of banking from a single place and at one time. Such provision requires not only a degree of multi-skilling but also very careful thought about the appropriateness and cost benefit of the level and duration of support to be offered. Will everything be answered or will complex enquiries be passed on to a pre-booked appointment with a more expensive specialist? Should the duration of help be time constrained in order to ensure maximum benefit for maximum numbers? Is there an underlying principle that students should be helped in such a way that it gives them a transferable skill?

Greater emphasis is being put on study skills training in most universities. Schemes currently vary between generic, cross institutional programmes through to discipline specific training. Sometimes such provision is firmly in the curriculum and assessed but often the surrender of time is resisted by the discipline. Formats vary between generic work books through to full blown taught sessions and, increasingly, the provision of home pages and multimedia packages. Responsibility for the creation of materials and the delivery of learning varies between academics and librarians, often and increasingly in happy cooperation. Alongside this lies the provision of more detailed guidance/navigation to learning resources specific to the student's discipline, course or even course component regardless of medium. These are most frequently print on paper or campus net mounted.

Skills: (in addition to a wide knowledge of the facilities and resources) interpersonal, teaching/tutorial, negotiation and customer care. Design, creation and delivery of learning materials, teaching and interpersonal, educational administration and publishing.

Conclusion

The implications for the management of staff development which will equip us with the necessary skills are, or course, not very easy. For the same reasons that our institutions are becoming learner centred and are facilitating independent learning, our staff development efforts are likely to be most effective if they:

- are designed in advance against clear and understood learning objectives;
- consciously balance the acquisition of theoretical principles with skills enhancement and reinforcement;
- are largely based upon project work and learning by doing, chiefly in groups (of particular importance are those joint development projects which allow the growth of understanding between academic and academic support staff);
- advance departmental and institutional functions that reflect the needs and abilities of individuals and teams (there are clearly links with appraisal here – see Chapter 3);
- support individuals in accepting delegated authority;
- are linked to the world outside, the library and the institution where relevant;
- mimic the learning experienced by service customers as this gives a particularly useful resonance.

Reference

1   Gibbs, Graham *et. al.*, *Institutional support for resource based learning*, Oxford, Oxford Centre for Staff Development, 1994.

6

The Context of Convergence

PROFESSOR MEL COLLIER

What is convergence?

Convergence is such a topical issue at present in British universities that it is tempting to believe that there is a common understanding of what convergence means. A quick glance at published opinion on the topic, however, shows that such a belief would be unfounded. It is not surprising therefore that as a common understanding is lacking, the advisability of convergence is a controversial or even polemical issue. This is illustrated by the now famous letter to the *Times Higher Education Supplement* by Ratcliffe and Hartley in March 1993[1] and the subsequent replies.[2, 3] The continuing interest in the topic was amply demonstrated by the lively and humorous yet serious debate held at the UCISA/SCONUL/AHUA 4th Joint Conference at Cranfield University in September 1995, and by the special issue of *Relay*, the Journal of the University, College and Research Group of the Library Association.[4]

Analysis of the arguments adduced in the correspondence, literature and debate identifies a number of themes. The first theme emphasizes the need for a customer service culture in which students receive the services they need, irrespective of the professional and management structures which lie behind those services but which are of little interest to the students. This theme is articulated clearly by Sidgreaves[5] and Slater.[6] Another theme focuses on management and the extent to which the range of skills and services offered in community support services can be managed within a single structure. At one end of the scale is the view that technical interrelationships are so intimate that services should be managed within multi-talented structures, a view expressed quite some time ago by Battin.[7] At the other is the view that priorities and management needs in diverse bodies, such as computing services and libraries, are incompatible, the view expressed by Ratcliffe and Hartley.

A third theme, related to the second but distinct from it, is that of professional culture. Many hours of debate have been spent on asserting (for it is always assertion) that this professional group or the other displays such and such characteristics. This is perhaps the least helpful topic of debate as it is based on generalizations and usually reflects divisive position-taking by professional groups. Finally there is the resource theme which can be argued two ways. If like Smith[8] you do not agree with convergence you might see it as a threat to the resource base of a particular service, or if like Lovecy[9] you are favourable you will see convergence as an opportunity to achieve overall economies in the institution and reduction of internal competition for resources.

Such themes as these, and no doubt there are others which could be added, illustrate the fact that the convergence debate often descends into mechanisms, structures and turf rather than a clarification of what is meant by convergence and why it is important. First, let us understand that convergence is not primarily about structures, which are secondary and subservient to it. It follows that there is no single structural configuration which is right. Convergence is one of the most tangible manifestations of the changing nature of higher education which, in Britain and Australia particularly, has been subjected to radical reforming pressure over recent years. This pressure has resulted in major expansion of opportunity, huge increases in flexibility, and an emphasis on choice and quality which was unknown not so long ago. Fiscal policy meanwhile has tightened relentlessly and demographic change has produced new market demands. Convergence must be seen therefore as part of the re-orientation of higher education to a radically different market environment as we approach the millennium. Therefore, we define convergence as:

> the process of strategic re-alignment of learning and research support activities to provide more effective customer services in the changing teaching and learning environment.

This definition lifts the discussion out of narrow structural or professional concerns and ensures that changes are customer driven not staff oriented. Of course, as solutions emerge from the re-alignment process, restructuring invariably follows and traditional professional groupings and allegiances break down, perhaps for ever or perhaps to be replaced by new identifiable groupings. Whichever is the case, it is apparent that convergence is a key consideration for staff development in academic libraries, both to aid staff through periods of transition and to help them develop the competency profiles which will be required to operate effectively in the new situation.

History of convergence

It is now some eight years since the first institutions of higher education in the UK took the important step of implementing convergence in their major academic services. Over a two-year period, Plymouth, Salford and Stirling brought various combinations of services under a single manager and a number of other institutions put convergence in a variety of guises into their agendas. In the case of De Montfort University, a merger of computing services and the library took place in September 1989 followed by the amalgamation of the media centre in 1992. As has been pointed out[10] convergence at that time was not a new idea, having been championed particularly in the United States, the idea going hand-in-hand with the concept of the electronic campus. Practical experience was, however, still thin on the ground and certainly not well documented. Post hoc reviews containing serious evaluations are scarce.[11]

Many other institutions might now claim to be engaged in convergence in some shape or form. Whether what is happening is a strategic process along the lines of our definition is however debatable. Certainly some new structures are emerging but although structures are of intense interest to professionals they are only a means to an end. In assessing the current position of convergence it is worth examining the rationales behind the changes which started to take place in the mid to late 1980s. A number of themes can be identified from the literature of the time. Perhaps the most dominant[12] is that information technologies, educational technologies and information services were becoming so intertwined that the relevant technical and management skills available to the institutions should be harnessed together. We call this the *technocratic imperative* argument.

Then there was the view that the strategic and economic implications of IT, information and media services for the success of institutions were so great that clear and simple lines of authority should be established in order to ensure sound decision making informed by institutional strategic intelligence. We call this the *executive thrust* argument.[13]

The next theme is based on the realization that a university is a knowledge based organization which is both a consumer and an originator of information.[14] Its stock-in-trade is the universe of recorded knowledge to which it adds year on year through its own research. As a player in an increasingly competitive market the university also needs to manage its corporate information efficiently. These three types of information require an identifiable focus of professional expertise which adds up to what we call the *information management* argument.

Finally, within this group of management orientated issues, is the fact that severally, these services consume a substantial amount of institutional resource and, if not merged, are inevitably in competition. The sum of the resource in a converged service is likely to be greater than the sum of the separate parts and convergence provides the opportunity for more efficient usage of resource. This we characterize as the *resource management* argument.[15]

These management-orientated arguments can be contrasted with the user-orientated perspective which can be called the electronic scholar argument, perhaps most notably promulgated by Battin[16] and boosted in the United States by the Wingspread Conference[17] and in the UK by the Banbury Conference.[18] This argument characterizes the student and academic as information navigators roaming the global networks and interacting with information resources to enrich their teaching and learning experience. Whilst we can all now relate readily to that scenario, it is interesting to note that the convergence literature of the time pays little or no attention to technology in teaching and learning. Convergers appeared to be focused on electronic information sources but not on courseware and the process of teaching and learning as they are much more today.

Understandably, the rationales and motivations behind convergence in the mid to late 1980s were the management and structural issues which are important to professionals seeking to do a competent job in times of impending change. Even the electronic scholar model appears to have been primarily a transposition of the library into the desktop rather than an examination of how teachers teach and how learners learn, and how converged services impact on those processes. If there have been impacts on teaching and learning from convergence they have been outcomes which were not clearly envisaged or indeed intended at the time.

Current position of convergence

UK in relation to other countries

Currently in the UK well over 30 institutions appear to be involved in convergence and no doubt many more are considering it. As we have noted above, convergence is a very live issue in the UK with similar movements taking place in Ireland and Australia. Interestingly, although the earliest published ideas were in the United States, those early initiatives do not as far as one can tell from the literature appear to have multiplied, and at least one notable case has regressed. This tends to be confirmed in informal discussions with American colleagues. Several reasons could be suggested. For instance, it is arguable that the reduction in unit of resource has not yet reached a stage in the United States where it has provoked a radical response, and also that faculty and professional structures are so strong relative to the executive that institutional change is not easily effected by strategic measures. Crossing the Channel to continental Europe, convergence appears to be largely unknown and descriptions of recent British developments tend to evoke expressions of surprise. This could be explained in Northern Europe, where information technology in libraries is well developed, by the fact that there have not been significant radical pressures on universities sufficient to provoke change, and in Southern Europe by the fact that information technology in libraries tends not to be sufficiently developed for the issue to be raised at all. Returning to the case of the UK it is clear that major change agents are influencing convergence within the overall financial, demographic and market forces we have already mentioned.

Not least is the series of initiatives from the funding councils which seek to bring about change in the system by top slicing funds and inviting universities to bid against defined criteria. The Teaching and Learning Technology Programme (TLTP) which commenced in 1992 is producing its first deliverables at this time. Its aim was to achieve efficiencies in teaching and learning through new technology and to produce deliverables which are transferable throughout the sector, with a considerable emphasis therefore on cooperation. The methodology was rough and ready, brevity of proposals being regarded as a virtue. By distributing substantial amounts of money to cooperative and institutional projects, it is hoped that efficiencies and good practice will be embedded throughout the sector. Whilst it is too early to assess the deliverables it is clear that an early beneficial outcome is the creation of a climate of change in teaching and learning and a focus on educational technology on an unprecedented scale.

This approach symbolizes the culture of competition, tempered by cooperation, within which we work and where strategic interventions are made via funding initiatives. On a smaller scale, the Joint Information Systems Committee (JISC) new technology initiatives, perform the same functions. The funding councils are not the only agents of change. The Enterprise Learning Initiatives have been funded by the Department of Employment with the general aim of helping institutions produce graduates who are better prepared for the world of work. The emphasis is on learning outcomes, competences, skills and personal transferable skills.

Impacts on teaching and learning

Perhaps we should take as our starting point the electronic scholar envisaged in the early 1980s, and consider to what extent that has been realized. Connectivity for researchers to the campus network and then to the Joint Academic Network (JANET) and the Internet is now commonplace, although the level of connectivity must vary considerably between institutions, and within institutions between locations and disciplines. Clearly there has been a significant impact on the learning processes and research habits of researchers who have access to list servers, bulletin boards and the Internet facilities and it is safe to say that the opportunities of the Internet, information navigation and peer communications, have set in motion changes which are irreversible.

Turning to first degree and other taught programmes, convergence has clearly provided a hospitable environment. Staff with complementary skills are available to help students at service points with information, media and IT problems. IT resources for student-centred study and assignment preparation are proliferating rapidly. Media, IT and library services are collaborating to create good quality materials to support the learning process.

The impact on taught courses however is very much at a formative stage. Although technology-based training has proved to be highly successful in certain well-structured industrial training contexts, computer-based learning has not yet transferred on any scale into taught programmes. A huge boost has been given by the TLTP but the deliverables are only just becoming available. Within most, if not all universities, there are pockets of activity and individual project work but widespread embedding is not yet in evidence. Convergence has provided the environment for increasing pervasiveness of computer based learning, but it would be premature to construe direct links between convergence and fundamental change in learning methods. The link will only be apparent when media and computer-based learning products are adopted into mainstream degree programmes on a significant scale. Two major changes need to take place in order to provoke this: first the introduction on a significant scale across the university of open or resource based learning into full-time undergraduate programmes, and secondly the much heralded arrival of large scale computer mediated study part-time by distance learning.

Taking the national view, therefore, we can observe the trends and remark that teaching and learning is in a considerable state of flux. It is not safe, however, to assume that activity is uniform across British universities, that convergence has made recurrent or consistent impacts or that a consistent picture of convergence itself is emerging.

Staff development issues

The emerging convergence model

From our definition it is clear that convergence must be a re-alignment of services and facilities to respond to changing customer needs. It takes place in a context where the library is just one among several agents providing services to users and where activities of all the agents overlap to the extent that continued separate development will be counterproductive, unhelpful or confusing to the users. The most convincing approaches to convergence appear to be those where services to users are looked at from the user point of view, deconstructed from their historic service structures and reassembled into more helpful constructs. At the University of Birmingham, for instance, activities of the Academic Computing Service, the Library and Television Services/Centre for Computer Based Learning have been reallocated to the five divisions of Learning and Research Support, Public Services, Collection Management, Information Systems and Administration. Perhaps the most significant element of this initiative is the aim to produce a consistent public service approach to customers across activities which were formally based in professionally or technically orientated groupings. Until now, convergence has been associated with the newer universities (we include those created in the 60s). That such a radical change should take place in a large, more traditional university like Birmingham is a significant indicator that something important is under way. The reconstructed components of the converged model will naturally vary to some extent according to the institution but a fully converged model would have the following characteristics:

- consistent one-stop approach to customer services
- avoidance of internal overlap or competition
- rationalized administration
- flexibility of resource allocation across services according to customer needs
- flexibility of human resource management across service areas
- integrated management
- breakdown of professional demarcations
- multi-disciplinary teams
- multi-talented staff.

The ultimate formulation of a converged service is therefore a service model in which customer need determines service configuration, resources can be allocated flexibly across all areas of activity and wasteful duplication or competition is avoided. Although, as we have said, revised structures cannot of themselves guarantee these benefits, it is hard to see how they can be provided without management restructuring. Those services which are merely brought together into one reporting line or which have a rotating chairperson approach cannot seriously be described as converged. Rotating chairpersons, service cooperation and shared line reporting at most are early stages on the road to convergence. In this respect we differ from Fielden[19] when he says that it is not necessary to have organizational convergence for operational convergence to happen. This is a fudge to allow for those situations where for political or other reasons real convergence has not happened.

Opportunities and competences

It will readily be recognized that the fully converged service has major implications for staff development. New teams will be created with a greater diversity of skills, and many staff will need help with adjusting their attitude to different colleagues, different tasks and new customers. In today's pervasive IT environment a range of skills including information, computing and educational media skills are devolving out to the end-user resulting in the possibility of perceived de-skilling of support staff. Support staff faced with this situation must re-skill in order to keep ahead of the end-users and maintain their indispensability. Rather than having *different* skills it may be a question of converged service staff having higher or more advanced skills than those of academics. The re-skilling process will be a never-ending cycle.

Removal of service boundaries is starting to have a noticeable effect on staff aspirations and career paths. Opportunities are now available for multi-faceted roles which some staff find stimulating and challenging. Computing services people are moving into courseware development and electronic library work. Media people are influencing strongly the design and development of courses. Librarians are moving into database development, courseware and open learning, quality management and academic staff development. In the wake of this, professional territories will also be re-drawn. In a fully converged service environment general insistence on particular professional chartships would become absurd. If librarians, computer scientists and educational technologists are working side by side in a multidisciplinary team, the important attributes are competences not professional labels. Chartships will only be useful in as far as they vouch for an individual's competences. Wise professional associations will be as expansive as possible in the definition of the professional competences which they embrace.

One is tempted to wonder where this process will end. Initially convergence was mostly about libraries re-aligning with computing services, but as we have seen, media, audiovisual, educational technology and staff development services are often now included. However, as the trend in higher education moves away from teaching-centred to learning-centred approaches and it is operationalized through technology-based, resource-based, open and distance learning methodologies, the distinction between those providing learning support services and those providing teaching services also becomes blurred. In a 'learning institution' the role of learning support becomes as important as teaching, leading to what Fielden calls academic convergence.

Staff development programmes

Customer care

It has become commonplace to emphasize the need for customer care and awareness and most staff know in theory that they have customers. However, it is easy in traditional structures and when under pressure to forget the dictum. In most universities bureaucracy is still alive and well, which aggravates the problem. In the type of customer-orientated converged service described above, the customer care ethic will have more chance of asserting itself than in services divided along professional lines. Nevertheless, pressure will intensify for staff to work according to best practice within the sort of policies inspired by the best examples from the retail and service industry sectors. A word of caution is added here, namely that the student–library relationship is not entirely analogous to the customer–retailer relationship. Students have an obligation to work within the rules and regulations of the library and will not always be right. Codes of good practice and student charters are essential to set the ground rules for effective operation of customer care policies. It is evident that customer care training will be an ongoing requirement at all levels of service from the formulation of policy by top management to the effective delivery and empowerment to deliver those services on the ground.

Culture change

We have touched earlier on the fact that much is made of the perceived differences in culture between the constituent professional groupings within converged services. We have observed that these perceptions are likely to be generalizations and based on anecdote, but whatever the facts, they are quite persistent. These perceptions will fade in time, as staff become accustomed to work together, but in a well managed environment, divisive issues like this cannot be allowed to fester and should be addressed in the staff development programme. An active staff development programme will itself break down barriers and establish common ground, but the issue of culture change, or *perception of culture difference*, could well be a specific objective of the programme, with relevant focused actions.

Re-skilling

In many ways the re-skilling of our staff is the most straightforward of the staff development issues. Once personnel have adjusted to new imperatives, new culture and a customer environment they will readily appreciate the need for training in new skills and most staff will be enthusiastic and capable. There could of course be casualties along the way. Where staff are unwilling or unable to accept change then there is a capability issue which must be handled sensitively within institutional policies and good practice, but it must be addressed or else a disservice is done to the individual and the institution. Where staff are willing but inept in acquiring new skills this is not so serious: in the fully converged service model there is such a range and diversity of skill requirement that it is hard to imagine that appropriate roles cannot be found. Fielden[20] suggests a few areas where operational convergence is manifest already: strategic planning, networking, joint IT facilities, user education. The report envisages a greater convergence in learning support. Specific skills which could be needed in the changing environment are too numerous to mention here and will vary considerably according to service profile, but it is obvious that the staff development programme will contain a range of skill-specific training activities. Staff will relate readily to these training opportunities, and the training programme will have a high approval rating if the choice and mix are right.

Management

At a superficial level, perhaps the most damaging criticism of convergence is that the activities of the various constituent services are so diverse that they should not be brought into one management structure or that management of such services could not be embraced by a single person. More mature reflection however shows that this argument is seriously flawed. If it were valid then major companies could not be run by accountants and university vice chancellors could not be professors of chemistry, both of which are manifestly untrue. This is not to say, however, that managing a converged service is not a formidable challenge. Staff development for middle and senior management is required to ensure that the standards of management expected of experienced professionals operating in their own domain are carried through as they progress into other domains. In a large converged ser vice some of the needs of the middle management in this respect could no doubt be accommodated by the in-house staff development programme, but at top level programmes organized by CVCP, Higher Education Funding Councils (HEFCs) or by the emerging group of heads of converged services are more appropriate.

Conclusion

Convergence is nearing the end of its first decade during which there have been many debates and experiences. It cannot be said, however, that the situation is stabilizing or that a coherent theory of the management and development of converged services is emerging. Convergence affects the considerable state of flux and turmoil within British higher education. Despite the controversy surrounding convergence it is evident that it is now a dominant factor in the development of learning support services and will not be reversed. The trend will be towards more convergence in institutions and it will increasingly be underpinned by management restructuring. Staff development is essential for successful implementation of structural and service change and programmes are needed to address four key issues: customer care, cultural change, re-skilling and management development.

Despite the variation and diversity of services implied within convergence it is time for a coherent theory to be developed to provide a framework for management and development of such services. This will build on and integrate the most relevant aspects of the management theory of the constituent services but it will also require new thinking by theorists and practitioners alike. When the context of convergence is more fully analysed and understood, the staff development programmes which are essential to the process of systemic change will be all the more effective.

References

1 Ratcliffe, F. and Hartley, D., Library Services [Letter], *Times Higher Education Supplement*, 5 Mar. 1993, 17.

2 Lovecy, I., Libraries IT role overdue? [Letter], *Times Higher Education Supplement*, 12 Mar. 1993, 12.

3 Crocker, P., [letter in same issue].

4 Library and Computing Services, 'Converge, merge or diverge?', *Relay*, (42), 1995.

5 Sidgreaves, I., 'Convergence – an update', *Relay*, (42), 1995, 3–6.

6 Slater, J., [Untitled contribution to] Responses to 'Convergence – an update', *Relay*, (42), 1995, 9.

7 Battin, P., 'The electronic library', *Collection management*, 9 (2/3), 1987, 133–41.

8 Smith, T., [Untitled contribution to] Responses to 'Convergence – an update', *Relay*, (42), 1995, 7–8.

9 Lovecy, I., [Untitled contribution to] Responses to 'Convergence – an update', *Relay*, (42), 1995, 7.

10 Bebbington, L. and Cronin, B., 'Courtship and competition on campus: the convergence of university libraries and computing centres', *Library review*, 38 (2), 1989, 7–16.

11 An example is: Revill, D., 'Learning resources provision and integration in an English polytechnic', *IATUL proceedings*, new series, (1), 1992, 23–32.

12 Arms, W. Y., and Michalak, T. J., 'The merger of libraries with computing at Carnegie Mellon University', *British journal of academic librarianship*, 3 (3), 1988, 153–64.

13 Kelly, P., 'Information management: an academic context', *British journal of academic librarianship*, 3 (3), 1988, 122–35.

14 Naylor, B., 'The convergence of the library and the computing service: the central issues', *British journal of academic librarianship*, 3 (3), 1988, 172–85.

15 Harris, C., 'Academic information services at the University of Salford', *British journal of academic librarianship*, 3 (3), 1988, 147–52.

16 Battin, *op. cit.*

17 Wingspread, Conference on information resources, *Campus of the future*, June 22–24, 1986. Dublin, Ohio, OCLC, 1987.

18 Brindley, L. J., 'The electronic campus: an information strategy', *Proceedings of a conference held at Banbury, 28–30 October 1988*, London, British Library Board, 1988.

19 Fielden Report, 15.

20 *Op. cit.*, 16.

7

Staff Development for Library Assistants

PHIL SYKES

Introduction

Scope of this chapter

This chapter looks at changes in the environment in which we are working and the effect these have upon the training and staff development needs of library assistants. Its primary aim is not to describe how we should train and develop staff. Rather it offers a perspective on where our training and development should be leading – in other words 'What are we developing people towards and what kind of world are we training them *for*?' First, the theme is introduced and some preliminary observations made, and then some broad contextual factors are examined – the pressure towards upskilling, the need to cope with constant change, and the trend towards team-based working – with discussion of possible training and development responses to these factors. The next section considers some topical matters and their staff development implications: convergence, the Internet, changes in teaching and learning and the move towards more customer-oriented services. The final section covers the management of development for library assistants and its place in our overall strategic management.

Follett and Fielden

Many of our current debates in academic librarianship spring from the recommendations of the Follett[1] and Fielden[2] reports. Follett is for staff development in the same way that it is against sin. It has little to say about it, except at a level of generality, and even less to say about the staff development needs of library assistants. Fielden covers staff development in detail, though its treatment of other topics under the 'Human Resource Management' umbrella – the acquisition, appraisal, reward and retention of staff – is, as Julie Parry argues, somewhat cursory.[3] Fielden, while ostensibly the missing staff development component of Follett, in fact reflects an entirely different world view from the parent report. Both reports have their (entirely different) merits. Follet is cautious and sober: it nudges the ship of progress forward without making too many waves. Its conservative tone was shrewdly calculated to influence vice-chancellors and funding councils. Fielden chances its arm more. In so doing it runs occasional risks with its credibility, and weakens its clout with the funders. Follett is less likely to be dramatically wrong. But it is also less likely to be prophetically right.

Although this chapter will try to avoid being a mere critical commentary on these sacred texts, many of the themes which it investigates spring from the Fielden Report. Paragraph references to the report are, therefore, given for the reader who wishes to consult the original.

The typical library assistant?

In order to make generalizations about the training needs of a particular group of staff it would be useful to be able to generalize about the common characteristics of that group. Davinson,[4] in a well known statement, drew attention to the 'homogeneity of interest and aim' that united all library staff before 1965 when the move towards an 'all-graduate' profession began, and laments the loss of that unity subsequently. It seems now, however, that, even within the sundered groups, that homogeneity is breaking down. Josephine Webb[5] draws attention to this heterogeneity in an article written in 1990, but over the last five years it has become an even more pronounced characteristic. Consider the following distinctions among the staff we bring together under the portmanteau term 'library assistant':

Graduate	Non-graduate
Eager for change	Prefer status quo
Temporary	Permanent
Part-time	Full-time

Daytime	Evening
Weekday	Weekend
One line job description (e.g. shelver)	Full job description
Agency staff	Direct employees

The practical consequence of this heterogeneity is, first, that any development programme has to take account of the level of prior training and knowledge of the different participants, and of the actual current and future demands of their jobs. If your assistants are a heterogeneous group, their training needs will not be homogeneous. Secondly, it reminds us of the need to plan for the training needs of those at the casual/part-time end of the spectrum. We may feel a warm glow of satisfaction at having provided regular weekly staff development sessions, but this will be of no use to part-time assistants who will never be present at the appointed time.

The broad context

Talk to almost any assistant who worked in an academic library in the 1960s or 1970s and you will hear an elegiac tone – a lament for a vanished world. Nor is this simply a matter of distance lending enchantment. Consider some recent changes:

- sharply declining unit of funding (requiring greater efficiency)
- competitive allocation of funding (leading to greater preoccupation with measurable quality)
- increasingly 'consumerist' approach to higher education
- declining membership and power of trades unions
- increased pressure to 'contract out' services
- computerization of office and library housekeeping routines
- digitization of bibliographic and full-text information
- enormous increase in student numbers.

Any of these changes could, individually, have altered the working life of our assistants considerably. Together they have wrought a revolution (and are still doing so as most of them are continuing rather than completed changes). What are some of the consequences of these changes for library assistants?

Upskilling

In various ways, the trends noted above have tended to increase the challenge and complexity of assistants' jobs. One of the first effects of financial stringency is to promote more delegation, and create a situation in which, as Mary Casteleyn says '. . . the greater exploitation of less qualified staff may well be a financial necessity'.[6] Organizations can no longer afford the luxury of allowing higher-graded members of staff to perform jobs which could be performed by the lower-graded. The general principle that jobs should be delegated to the lowest graded staff competent to perform them wins the day against the scruples of those who fear a slight decline in quality. Although, theoretically, these changes ought to be accompanied by upgrading, there is no evidence that this is universally the case. Except for a brief period in the 1980s, the experience of many employers in the Thatcher and post-Thatcher years is that they are in a buyer's market. The effects of the demographic time bomb, much talked about in the late 1980s and early 1990s, do not seem to be materializing.

At the same time as more complex tasks are being delegated to assistants, some of the simpler routines are dropping out of the bottom of their job descriptions. For some this is a consequence of contracting out. Those jobs which are contracted out tend to be those which are easiest to define and codify – in other words, repetitive and predictable tasks such as the clerical aspects of book processing, which are now often dealt with by library suppliers.

Automation and digitization, however, have done more than anything else both to eliminate routine tasks and to add additional areas of challenge to assistants' jobs. Despite the fears of de-skilling that were expressed in the late 70s and early 80s, automation of housekeeping has removed a great deal of drudgery and repetition from circulation work (and, incidentally, ensured that those circulation problems which do remain require considerable mental agility to solve!). The proliferation of electronic sources of information mean that, except where enquiries are jealously guarded by professionally qualified staff, library assistants tend to be exposed to a wider range of enquiries and demands upon their talents than they were a decade ago.

Constant change

'Change is inevitable' as someone observed, 'except with vending machines'. But change is not what it used to be. Libraries have always had to adapt, but few would deny that the pervasiveness and pace of change have increased dramatically of late. A life of calm diversified by turbulence has been replaced by a life of turbulence diversified by increasingly rare interludes of calm.

Obviously, where specific changes are being introduced, we need to provide training for them. But something more than this is needed, if we are to deal with changes of the magnitude described by Fielden. There is an old joke: 'How many therapists does it take to change a light bulb?'. The answer is 'One, but the light bulb really has to want to change'. The challenge for us is how we make our light bulbs want to change. How do we create libraries which are at ease with change – capable of changing and renewing themselves without external compulsion? How also, can we push the initiation of change down to a lower level? Because organizations where the initiation of change is the exclusive preserve of senior managers are unlikely to thrive in the 21st century.

Team-based staffing structures and flatter organizations

Fielden repeatedly emphasizes the importance of adopting team-based management structures – for instance subject teams and project teams – in order to cope with the challenges that lie before us (see for example Fielden 4.13). Certainly, as far as coping with change is concerned, subject teams have much to recommend them. They allow staff to derive their sense of stability and loyalty from identification with a particular client group rather than from identification with a particular set of routines and procedures (the approach to working identified by Charles Handy as a 'role culture'7). They also encourage a certain flexibility within teams as to who does what. All this makes change easier to cope with. It seems like a natural, organic adaptation to the shifting needs of a known group, rather than a painful and arbitrary abandonment of comfortingly familiar routines.

Project teams – formed to undertake particular tasks and disbanded when their work is done – are also predicted by Fielden to become increasingly common. Many libraries first adopted this way of working as a means of managing the automation of housekeeping, and were pleased with the results. They found that as well as helping automation to proceed smoothly it helped to secure acceptance of, and commitment to, the new systems being introduced.

This feeling of ownership of changes and policies is, perhaps, one of the most important benefits of the team approach. Managing in a way which secures the commitment and motivation of staff is now more important than it ever was. As organizations become flatter, and the span of discretion of each individual manager widens, it becomes less and less possible to ensure high quality work through close supervision and detailed direction. Conditions have to be created in which staff feel that they have a stake in, and a responsibility for, a particular area, and a reasonable opportunity to influence decisions made about it.

How do we respond to these broad changes?

So, we need upskilled assistants who are at ease with change and work creatively and comfortably within less hierarchical, more team-based structures. A key point to realize at the outset is what an inadequate instrument training and development is, on its own, to bring about changes of this magnitude. This point is explored more thoroughly in the concluding section of this chapter which places staff development in the context of the other factors necessary to organizational change.

Nevertheless it would be mere defeatism to neglect staff development simply because it is not an all-sufficient answer to our problems. Training and development may not be a sufficient condition for bringing about organizational transformation but it is a necessary one. If we take upskilling, for example, it is clearly better if we can identify the areas where skills need to be developed and the staff who need to develop them, rather than leaving this process to chance and the vagaries of individual managers' styles. As for encouraging change and adaptation, there are formal techniques at our disposal. Quality Circle training, for example, is an ideal way of getting staff used to the idea that they are able to initiate changes and are not merely 'Engines that move/ In predestinate grooves'. We can also help effective teams to form and develop. Subject teams may need to go through a 'getting to know you' stage which may be accelerated by abstracting the team from its everyday work and providing structured training in team building. In so far as interpersonal problems may be an obstacle to effective team working, such areas as assertiveness training may be of assistance. There are a variety of formal techniques which may assist project teams in their work: brainstorming and methods of comparing and refining different solutions to problems are obvious examples.

Some current concerns in academic librarianship

This section considers the training and development implications for library assistants of some particularly topical changes in libraries: convergence, the growth of the Internet, new approaches to teaching and learning, and the movement towards 'customer service' approaches.

Convergence

'To converge or not to converge?' is a hotly disputed question in UK higher education. Fielden sees it as both desirable and inevitable but this is by no means the consensus view (Fielden 2.25–2.31). From the point of view of analysing long-term staff development needs, however, it is not actually necessary to take sides in the debate. Convergence is simply an optional staging post in an obligatory journey. We are all travelling towards a future in which a significant proportion of information will be mediated in electronic form – not just bibliographic materials or esoteric research sources, but core undergraduate reading and essential courseware. Our libraries will clearly have to provide access to these materials, which students will want to download, print, and manipulate within applications software packages. Consequently all staff are going to need a considerably greater familiarity than they currently possess with microcomputer software and the workings of at least their local institutional networks. (This area is explored in depth in Chapter 6.)

The Internet

Whether all staff are going to need to navigate around external networks must be regarded as more of an open question, although Fielden seems to take this view when he says 'Almost universally staff will need to know how to access and navigate electronic databases'. Internet enthusiasts undoubtedly believe that undergraduates will be using the Internet to satisfy their core information needs in a very short time, and that all staff must, therefore, become accomplished 'surfers' too. There remain obstacles to the realization of this utopian vision – principally the existence of copyright law, and the continuing need of most serious information providers to make a profit. These inconvenient facts mean that the main electronic sources used by students on taught courses will continue to be items over which libraries have some form of ownership, either because they are mounted on internal networks or because they are subscription services accessed through well-defined gateways on our networks. Basic grade staff are going to need to know their way around their institution's own internal networks to guide users to these sources, and they are going to need to know how to get on to the Internet. It seems probable that a sophisticated mastery of external sources will continue to be a requirement only of more highly graded subject specialists.

New approaches to teaching and learning (Fielden 2.40–2.42)

The debate about the future of academic libraries has inevitably centred, of late, on the Follett and Fielden reports. It may yet be, however, that a third report, the MacFarlane report, turns out to have a more significant influence upon our future.[8] MacFarlane argues that institutions pay a huge price for courses which are independently designed by each lecturer and that the only economically feasible model for the future is to create, on a large scale, high quality courseware which is shared between a large number of organizations. Libraries move centre stage in the MacFarlane universe because, clearly, they are one of the principal locations from which courseware would be made available. If the changes advocated by MacFarlane take place they will have an enormous effect on subject support staff. Fielden argues that this will principally affect subject librarians. However, students will encounter both technical and intellectual difficulties with the use of networked learning software and they will turn for help to whoever is at hand. While it would be unreasonable to expect assistants to develop detailed pedagogical and subject knowledge, they will need to know something about the changes in learning delivery, be able to locate learning software on networks and deal with some of the recurring technical difficulties experienced by students in their use of learning software.

Customer service

Several sections of Fielden (see for example 2.48–2.50) encourage the adoption of more responsive and customer-oriented attitudes on the part of libraries. Since the public face of the library is, for many students, the assistants they see daily, it is tempting to assume that adoption of Fielden's recommendations will substantially alter the staff development needs of assistants. Certainly, 'Training in customer service skills and associated questions of inter-personal behaviour' (Fielden, section 4.38) is particularly, if not exclusively, relevant to assistants.

It is, however, instructive, to look more closely at section 2.48 where Fielden unpacks the notion of customer service. In it, there are two general references to the need for training, but when he defines the specifics of what needs to be done he talks first of soliciting feedback through questionnaires, surveys, informal meetings, focus groups and user committees. He then talks about the introduction of service improvement programmes, breaking this down into the following: carefully considered customer service policies; obtaining feedback; identifying quantitative and qualitative customer service standards; entering into service level agreements; and identifying ways of ensuring continuous service improvement. Assistants need to be aware of initiatives of this type, and to understand the reasons for them through appropriate training.

The future of staff development

The place of staff development in strategic management

Earlier, the point was made that organizational transformation on the scale envisaged cannot be brought about by staff development alone. It can only be one of a number of techniques at the organization's disposal in making itself team-based and change-friendly. A more comprehensive approach to cultural transformation is required. The philosophy encapsulated in the phrase 'Human Resource Management' (HRM) – incorporating as it does selection, appraisal, reward and development – takes us part of the way there. It is an obvious point, but one which may still be neglected by some libraries, that our selection procedures should work to select the same kinds of people that our staff development policies are working to develop. If, for example, our staff development policy for assistants places a premium on adaptability, customer sensitivity, and the ability to cope confidently and positively with change, then we should be alert to the inconsistency if our typical person specification gives a more exalted place to, say, previous experience, knowledge of current routines and attention to detail.

But even if our HRM strategy is internally consistent and impeccably forward-looking it will still fail in its objectives if it is out of line with the general mission, ethos and organizational structure of the library. There is no point, for example, in training up a cadre of self-starting and creative assistants, eager to work in participatively managed teams, if the real power structure of the organization is authoritarian and centralist, and middle and senior managers are expected to manage in a dully prescriptive and mechanistic way.

The management of staff development

When we think of staff development we still, all too often, think exclusively in terms of a series of formal training events in which staff are taken away from their everyday work and taught new skills. We think of it as something extraordinary – apart from our normal working lives: we are either 'on' duty, or 'off' on a training course. Perhaps this conception of training as an extraordinary phenomenon hangs on because, despite the evidence to the contrary, we still instinctively think of change as an extraordinary phenomenon – a kind of natural catastrophe which should not, by rights, befall us more than once in a generation.

Just as change has become commonplace, however, so must training be. Certainly, when we make changes we must, as Fielden advocates, consciously plan for the people who are to implement them (Section 3.33). But it is more than just a matter of willing the training means to achieve the management ends. Training has to become more everyday, humdrum, a more natural and easy part of our daily activities and more thoroughly woven in to our habits of thought.

In order to achieve this we must first ensure that our view of staff development encompasses more than just external courses and formal skills training. These need to be supplemented by, for example, mentoring, action learning, and placements and exchanges.

Secondly, we have to seek ways of delivering our programmes

cost-effectively and with minimum dislocation to the organization. This last point is particularly important for the training of assistants. One of the iron laws of librarianship is that – in the short term at least – a person's indispensability is inversely proportional to his or her seniority: users are unlikely to bewail the absence of senior managers, but woe betide you if your interlibrary loans assistant is away! Open and resource-based methods of learning, which can be taken up as time permits will be particularly valuable here, partly because they obviate the need to release large number of assistants for training simultaneously.

Thirdly, we need to capitalize on the staff development potential of our everyday transactions – of all the informal opportunities we have for moulding and developing staff. Staff briefing meetings, for example, may not be primarily conceived as staff development events, but they offer an ideal opportunity for communicating a sense of organizational development and purpose. In rapidly evolving organizations they can be an invaluable opportunity to describe 'the big picture'.

Perhaps one final aspect of the management of training that needs to be discussed is the assessment and acknowledgement of competences. As the tasks undertaken by assistants become more demanding and varied, we need a means of recording what our staff are competent to do – for our own internal planning purposes, as a morale booster, and as objective proof of competence to potential future employers. For Fielden, the 'Holy Grail' here lies in Scottish/National Vocational Qualifications (S/NVQs) (section 4.51–4.60). However, doubts are being expressed. The amount of bureaucracy associated with S/NVQs is off-putting and, more fundamentally, problems are being encountered with the whole notion of assessing competences with only minimal attention to the underpinning knowledge which contextualizes and makes sense of these competences. In some ways it may be that competences – as opposed to underpinning knowledge – date too quickly now to be usefully certifiable. Suppose S/NVQs had been introduced ten years ago; of what value would 'Browne issue' competences have been after the transition to automated systems?

Conclusion

We have lived through enormous changes in the last few years, and the pace of change shows no sign of slackening. Although staff development cannot, by itself, enable us to cope successfully with change, it will be a vital component in our response to it. It will be needed to equip staff with the skills and competences they require. Less obviously, it will be, for every academic library, one of the ways in which the organization interprets and explains itself to itself. This function is particularly important for staff without professional qualifications. Professionally trained staff have, or should have, the means of updating themselves and gaining an understanding of the changing context in which they are working. Library assistants do not have the same opportunities. The rapid evolutions and adaptations libraries have to undertake can be deeply disorientating to them.

We are witnessing a tremendous opening up of opportunities for libraries. The consensus about what an academic library actually *does* is, to a considerable extent, breaking down. Each library has to invent and reinvent itself to respond to the particular demands of the organization it serves. This could be exhilarating, but, without adequate preparation and management, it will be a traumatic experience, particularly for assistants. It can all too easily appear to them that our policies are merely – to borrow a phrase from our most famous poet-librarian – '. . . bent in / By the blows of what happened to happen'.[9] It is our responsibility to ensure that the disappearance of the old certainties does not leave a vacuum. Staff training and development is at least one of the ways in which we can provide that vital sense of direction and purpose.

References

1   *Follett report.*
2   *Fielden report.*
3   Parry, J., 'Supporting expansion: the future for library and information staff', *British journal of academic librarianship*, **9** (3), 1994, 149–66.
4   Davinson, D., 'Non-professional library staff education: a state of the art report and proposals for the future'. In *Studies in library management*, (7), London, Bingley, 1982, 39.
5   Webb, J., 'The non-professional in the academic library: education for para-professionalism', *Personnel training and education*, **7** (2), 1990, 22.
6   Casteleyn, J., 'Affiliated membership: land of cream and honey', *Personnel*

training and education, **8** (2), 1991, 38.
7   Handy, C., *Understanding organisations*, Harmondsworth, Penguin, 3rd edn, 1985, 190.
8   Committee of Scottish University Principals., *Teaching and learning in an expanding higher education system* (The MacFarlane Report), Midlothian, Polton House Press, 1992.
9   Larkin, P., *The Whitsun weddings: poems by Philip Larkin*, London, Faber and Faber, 1964, 43.

8

Staff Development for Subject Librarians

ROBERT BLUCK

The subject librarian's role

After initial experiments in the 1960s, subject librarians have become widely employed in both old and new universities and in other large academic libraries. There is a substantial literature on the role of subject librarians – though very little on their staff development. They have many titles and a variety of roles in different institutions. But the defining feature is that the subject librarian (or information specialist, or department librarian, or course resources officer) concentrates on the information needs of a specific group of students and staff.

Allowing for considerable variation between institutions and between subjects, the role is centred on four main areas: academic liaison, collection development, information skills teaching and enquiry work.

Academic liaison includes formal and informal meetings with teaching staff, to support curriculum development and course planning, and to discover and inform the information needs of students and staff. This is where the cycle of subject work begins. Liaison often involves regular subject or course meetings, where subject librarians will receive advance notice of new teaching proposals, and will be able to promote (and sometimes defend) library services. As library ambassadors, they need to be diplomatic and positive with academic staff, while not transferring loyalty away from their library base.

Collection development (or stock selection and editing) involves deciding what books, journals and electronic databases to purchase, within a given budget, to meet the information needs of the client group. Some recommendations come from academic staff through reading lists and research requests, but subject librarians often have to choose much of the material themselves. Collection development policies vary with the teaching and research role of the institution. Some old universities retain a greater archival role, while others, together with the new universities and HE college libraries, concentrate on access to current information. Policies for the withdrawal of little-used material are needed in all but the largest libraries.

Information skills teaching (or user education, or library instruction) can include everything from initial induction sessions to detailed work on literature searching with final year or research students. Guidance in using subject-based electronic sources such as CD-ROM is increasingly common. The information skills programme will vary between institutions, and between subject areas in the same institution, depending on the support of academic staff and the interest and enthusiasm of individual subject librarians. It may extend beyond traditional boundaries to include more general study skills work. Ideally these sessions are built into the curriculum to encourage students to attend and take an active part in the programme.

Enquiry work (or information work) may be on an individual subject basis, at a faculty level, or on a general enquiry desk where all subjects are dealt with. Individual patterns depend on the range of subjects taught, the numbers and deployment of subject staff, and the physical layout of libraries. Subject librarians will usually spend timetabled periods at enquiry desks where they often face interesting, challenging or obscure questions. An unusual blend of skills is needed here, from subject knowledge and an awareness of course requirements to interpersonal skills and some detective work.

Several other areas also form part of the subject librarian's role. Online searching is undertaken for information not available locally. Publicity is prepared to enable students and staff to locate the material they need easily, and to alert them to new publications. Short loan and special collections may be maintained, and there may be involvement in cataloguing and/or classification in a particular subject area.

The subject librarian has a key role to play in defining, selecting, acquiring and exploiting subject information. It is a popular role where staff can use their subject expertise, gain teaching experience, work closely with academic colleagues and have the satisfaction of helping students to become more confident in finding and using information. Subject librarians are often regarded with some envy by their function-based colleagues.

Subject librarians and career development

Some subject librarians are relatively comfortable with this attractive and varied role, though they are often under pressure due to the demands placed upon them. A few may even be too comfortable, perhaps wary of rapid change, or reluctant to develop new skills to adapt to new challenges. But many of them can become frustrated by the pressure of change and the lack of career prospects, and may feel that they are not getting the right experience to be considered for promotion when opportunities do arise.

It is widely held that subject librarians tend not to be able to acquire the appropriate experience for further promotion. Quiney[1] sees 'a basic conflict between the subject role and the functional role', where subject librarians do not gain sufficient management experience, and feel that they are only involved in management decision-making by virtue of other roles such as site responsibilities. Higginbottom[2] argues that the 'lack of any administrative or managerial functions among subject librarians . . . leads to a serious gap in the managerial chain.' Thompson and Carr[3] underline the point that subject librarians have less chance to show their administrative ability, which limits their promotion prospects.

At present, career prospects are limited for all academic librarians, both through internal promotion and transfer between institutions. Subject librarians may be further restricted by the structure of the library staffing establishment. Functional posts may lead logically from one level to another, for example from systems librarian to head of technical services, but there are only a few subject-based senior posts, mainly restricted to sub-librarians in old universities.

When promotion is available to the subject librarian, it is more likely to involve a joint role combining subject and management responsibility, based either on subject work (for example as Faculty Librarian) or on location (often as Site Librarian). Further promotion from these joint roles is almost always to a 'management-only' role, either as a traditional deputy librarian, or increasingly as a senior manager, one of several service heads who form a senior management team, led by the Librarian or Director of Information Services.

Although it is unrealistic for all subject librarians to expect to be library managers, their considerable and highly relevant expertise is sometimes neglected in their current role. Higginbottom[4] points out that because subject librarians are at the front end of the library service, with important contacts, 'it is essential that they should play a full part in planning, policy-making and budgeting'. This will enable them to provide information on user needs, and bring improved motivation through being able to influence library objectives. It will also enable them to gain some of the management skills that they need.

The Fielden Report and the need for change

The subject librarian's role is far from being static. It has changed rapidly in recent years, in response to new forms of information and new methods of teaching and learning. Increased student numbers have spread existing subject staff more thinly; widening modes of access have brought in more part time students; more student-centred learning demands a greater range of teaching skills; and the explosion of electronic information (from CD-ROM to the Internet) requires continuous updating of knowledge and skills. Convergence between libraries and computer centres may also broaden the academic liaison role to include the IT needs of students and staff. Continued financial constraints have placed greater pressure on collection development policies, and given impetus to the moves towards more networked information in electronic format.

These new demands upon subject librarians are emphasized in the recent Fielden Report,[5] which argues that in the context of greater convergence between libraries and computer centres, with universal network access and improved support for learners, the subject librarian's role will change and require new skills.

Fielden found a very wide range of practice in the subject librarian role. It may concentrate on ordering, classifying and cataloguing, or on 'close working with academic colleagues in a wide range of support activities', or even on research activity (in large research institutions). Fielden feels that the second of these three interpretations is the way in which the role will develop in future, and describes the essential areas as: course planning; study skills tuition (including assessment); academic audit and quality assurance; helping academic staff to understand the available resources; providing technical support, such as database access; assisting students; and producing educational material.

Fielden's investigations found an uneven pattern of academic liaison, with 'some remarkable examples of subject librarians playing a formative role in course design and contributing to faculty courses on study skills', but by contrast there were 'many more cases where the liaison is weak.' Subject librarians are increasingly expected to take on a larger 'learner support' role which 'ranges from user education and mediated database access to information skills education, and from mediated library-based tasks to tutorial support.' This strongly implies that subject librarians need much more than subject knowledge to perform effectively.

Two of Fielden's 'four key areas of change' in terms of staffing patterns and competences relate specifically to subject librarians. Firstly they will have 'a major para-academic role . . . as the initial mediators and facilitators of resource-based open learning, with responsibilities for first-line instruction and supervision of students.' Secondly the changes due to 'new technology and information systems' mean that 'all subject/information librarians will be expected to master "navigational skills" to get through electronic databases and show others how to do so.'

The other two key areas are more general, but relate to subject librarians as much as to other staff. Services will need to be more closely tailored to the needs of library customers; and making these changes 'will require new forms of operation and organization . . . working within services with a greater emphasis on team working and less on traditional hierarchical forms of working. . .'

All these projected changes have implications for subject librarians and their professional development. They will need to acquire more sophisticated teaching skills, further IT skills, a better understanding of the information needs of students and staff, and the ability to work creatively in subject-based teams rather than in isolation.

Subject librarians provide a vital link with the institution's academic programmes, but they are an expensive resource, and need to be used effectively to justify the considerable funding spent on them. This does not just mean adequate training (though of course it should be provided). An integrated staff development programme is needed to ensure that subject librarians continue to perform well in their current role, and that they are prepared for change and new challenges when they arrive.

Priorities and coordination

Staff development priorities suggest an inevitable tension between individual aspirations and the needs of the organization. Subject librarians may wish to acquire relevant management skills and experience to increase the prospects of promotion, while the library needs them to update their existing skills to enable them to cope with changes in the present role.

Jordan and Jones[6] argue that while individual and organizational needs may be different – 'managers have an obligation to help their staff reach full potential, even if this means they eventually lose them on promotion to another organization.' In practice this may be difficult to achieve, as staff development budgets are often limited, and there is considerable pressure on the existing service. Funding and time have to be weighed carefully against the advantages of any particular development activity.

Individual aspirations must be reconciled with the objectives of both the library and the parent institution. Unless the library is extremely well-funded, a staff development policy which allows all the subject librarians substantial time and funding to do research degrees is in danger of neglecting library objectives. However, a policy which limits them strictly to the immediate needs of the existing role (such as short IT skills courses) has become a training programme rather than a development policy. There has to be a genuine balance here, with both individual and organizational needs taken into account.

The subject librarian and the library need not be at odds, as the development of existing skills to improve liaison, library collections, information skills teaching and enquiry work, can be managed in such as way to benefit both the individual and the organization. To achieve this requires both coordinated management of staff development, and a positive approach from the subject librarians themselves.

Fielden emphasizes the need for 'a comprehensive staff development and training policy and plan for all staff'. Individual training is of course required for updating a wide range of skills, from teaching and IT to budgeting and project management. But genuine development has to be seen as part of a coherent programme to improve subject librarians' performance.

Staff development for subject librarians is often arranged on a rather ad hoc basis, depending on available funding and individual interest rather than any strategic approach. Those who are enthusiastic, persuasive and persistent tend to be the staff who gain funding and time off to pursue external courses. (They may also be the ones who eventually gain promotion, though as we have seen this usually means a move away from subject librarianship.) But what about experienced subject librarians who feel no need for further study? How are they to avoid professional stagnation, and how can they maintain their commitment and performance levels?

One possible model is to encourage (or even to require) subject librarians to gain specific qualifications, either before appointment or as post-entry training. This may be attempted at recruitment, where advertisements plead for applicants with a science degree. But it is rarely carried forward into a staff development programme. If library assistants are expected to acquire the City & Guilds Certificate or the Certificate in Management Studies (CMS) or the new S/NVQs, should subject librarians also be expected to gain a post-entry qualification to develop their knowledge and skills? This might be a subject degree, a teaching certificate, an MA in Library Management, or a management course such as the Diploma in Management Studies (DMS) or Masters in Business Administration (MBA).

This would be an expensive approach, both in funding and time, especially for external courses which involve full fees and travelling. Limited staff development funding would make this impracticable, or only achievable at the expense of basic training for other staff. The benefits for the library may be intangible and difficult to quantify but so is the cost of having a group of underdeveloped and disillusioned subject librarians. A uniform approach will also be inappropriate, for subject librarians may already have research degrees or a teaching qualification and the mid-career MA or DMS may suit individual rather than organizational objectives.

A staff development policy needs to be flexible enough to address the varied qualifications, experience and aspirations of the subject librarians. The new colleague who asks for funding and time to pursue a PhD should understand the need for a balance between supporting individual and organizational objectives. The experienced colleague who feels that there is little left to learn should realize that staff development is not an option, but a requirement, in the context of rapid educational change.

After formulating an overall policy, a training needs analysis should be carried out for subject librarians, either as a separate exercise or as part of staff appraisal. This will discover in more detail what individual expressed needs are, and where the library needs particular staff to develop their knowledge or skills. Managers can then begin to look at specific elements which may be needed in a staff development programme for subject librarians.

Specific development needs

Many of Fielden's recommendations on training and staff development relate directly to subject librarians. They should improve their awareness of customer needs, their understanding of change management, and their interpersonal and team skills. More specifically, subject librarians need to develop IT navigational skills and teaching and learning skills to expand their support role to students and staff. They will increasingly need 'to become involved with assisting academic departments with both course design and the development of teaching materials'.

Academic librarians approached by Green and Clarke[7] suggested that the essential qualities or skills required for a subject librarian were: IT skills and awareness; interpersonal skills (with library users and with colleagues); presentational skills (for teaching programmes); and team working. These all scored higher than subject knowledge. Perhaps these are the areas on which staff development programmes (and departments of librarianship) should be concentrating.

Other development needs may be grouped for the sake of convenience into four broad areas: management development (including an understanding of the educational context and change management), communication with customers (awareness of customer needs as well as development of teaching and IT skills), communication with colleagues (interpersonal and team skills) and professional and personal development. All these areas need to be built into a staff development programme which is comprehensive, affordable, deliverable and geared to the needs of both the library services and the individual subject librarian.

Development programmes

Management development

Subject librarians sometimes assume that management means managing people, and so may not appreciate the experience they are gaining in their current role. Managing library services for a specified group of customers should encourage them to develop their understanding of the educational context, through liaison with academic staff. Collection development enhances subject, bibliographic and budgeting skills. Information skills work helps to develop teaching and IT skills. Enquiry work provides an opportunity to learn more about customer needs and ways of responding to them.

It is also important for subject librarians (especially those who qualified some time ago) to grasp the principles that underlie good management practice. Human relations management is as important as organization theory, to encourage an understanding of motivation, leadership skills and conflict management. An understanding of change management is also needed.

As Veaner[8] points out, rapid technological and social change is an important factor in staff development. Staff need to be able to see beyond their everyday work to understand the context in which their contribution is being made. Some of the institutional context may be gleaned through academic liaison, and active involvement in committee work. They also need to keep up to date with broader institutional developments through the university or college newsletter, and with national developments through *The Times Higher Education Supplement* and the professional and educational press.

Communicating with customers

An awareness of customer needs should influence everything that the subject librarian does. This awareness can be achieved through academic liaison, involvement in course planning, and student feedback via course committees. The subject librarian must have a responsive attitude to changing needs, together with a knowledge of and ability to use appropriate monitoring and evaluative techniques.

Students often want subject librarians to find each piece of information for them, and there is a certain satisfaction in spoonfeeding them. But they need to be encouraged to discover things for themselves and to develop the transferable skill of becoming independent information handlers. A few demanding students can take up a great deal of time, and the subject librarian needs to practise effective time management to be able to provide a full range of library services to the whole client group.

Subject librarians have always been involved in teaching students in one form or another, but relatively few of them are really confident in this area. A few tutor librarians spend much of their time teaching, but for many staff it tends to be sporadic and the level of skill does not always develop beyond the rudimentary. They will inevitably be measured against their teaching colleagues in terms of knowledge and delivery, and an amateur approach will reflect poorly on the library service. Subject librarians need to be confident in a range of teaching techniques, for example, for large and small group work.

The development of IT skills should also be linked to customer needs. As well as acquiring the skills to operate systems and navigate through databases, subject librarians need to understand the wider context of how the information in their field is developing, and whether new CD-ROMs or Internet access tools are relevant to their staff and students. This is a rapidly moving and confusing area at present, which requires both enthusiasm and restraint, if time and funding are to be used effectively.

Communicating with colleagues

Effective cooperation with other library staff is as important for the subject librarian as developing a good rapport with customers. Quality of service can often depend on the interpersonal skills used in communicating with colleagues. Individuals need to assess their own strengths and weaknesses in such areas as listening skills, dealing with conflict, and being aware of the opinions and problems of their colleagues and be open to training designed to develop effective attitudes.

A team approach for subject services is suggested by

Higginbottom[2] and Fielden.[5] Leading a subject team provides a chance to gain staff management experience, and involvement in general library management. Adair[9] describes the threefold purpose of a team approach as 'achieving the task, building and maintaining the team, and developing the individual.' The additional team dimension may help to resolve tensions between the aspirations of the individual subject librarian and the needs of the organization.

Bluck[10] describes how the University of Northumbria adopted a team approach to reinforce commitment to common objectives, improve communication, and promote a more participative management style. This was prompted partly by subject librarians who felt isolated from the management process, and who wished to make a more positive contribution through increased responsibility and decision-making.

Skills in team building and team management, to enable staff to understand team goals and to work in a more cooperative and mutually supportive way are needed for this approach.

Professional and personal development

Conyers[11] argues that subject librarians 'need to maintain contact with other professionals', should continue with professional reading, and take an 'active role in professional activities at national or local level'. Library managers should encourage subject librarians to participate in LA groups such as the University, College and Research Group (UC&R) and the Colleges of Further and Higher Education Group (COFHE), and in subject groups such as the SCONUL Science & Technology Group. Each provides a forum for the exchange of experience and ideas, and a chance to meet colleagues to discuss common problems and give mutual support. The groups often generate their own speakers, where staff can gain experience of presenting material to colleagues.

Some subject librarians seem to read very little about librarianship, due to pressure of work or even lack of interest. Libraries should acquire relevant books and journals as staff development tools, in the same way as academic staff expect materials on teaching methods. Staff should be encouraged to read professional literature as an essential part of their work, rather than an optional interest.

Personal development, for example, where staff take courses

mainly for their own interest is only indirectly related to work. Subject librarians may wish to continue academic study in their own field, or pursue other subject-related interests. This can lead to opportunities for development through publication or giving conference papers.

The library is often unable to support such activities unless they relate directly to the current post but staff aspirations and interests should at least be considered. Perhaps fees cannot be paid, but hours can be rearranged to allow the subject librarian to attend lectures.The broad view of staff development is that it relates to the person as a whole and not only to their work.

Conclusion

The subject librarian is a vital element in the academic library, and the role remains popular and attractive despite the frustrations of professional stagnation.

Academic libraries need to support a coherent staff development programme for subject librarians, taking into account the changing role outlined in the Fielden Report, and recognizing the need to update subject and other skills. The programme should include the educational context of the subject librarian's work as well as management theory and practice. The emphasis throughout should be on communicating both with customers and colleagues, and the skills needed to expand the role in supporting client groups. These include IT skills, teaching skills, interpersonal and team working skills. Professional activities and reading should also be encouraged, together with personal development.

A cooperative balance is needed between the aspirations of the subject librarian and the objectives of the library. The individual needs to remain positive and realistic, continuing to develop in his or her current role, rather than constantly seeking promotion. Library managers should recognize the unique character of the subject librarian's role, and involve him or her in the management of the library. A genuine partnership between the self-motivated subject librarian and the participative organization is needed to maintain service standards, and to provide extended support for students and staff.

References

1   Quiney, L., 'The social sciences, business, management and law'. In Fletcher, J. (ed.), *Reader services in polytechnic libraries*, Aldershot, Gower, 1985, 62–94.

2   Higginbottom, J., 'The subject librarian. In Revill, D. (ed.), *Personnel management in polytechnic libraries*, Aldershot, Gower, 1987, 155–174.

3   Thompson, J. and Carr, R., *An Introduction to university library administration*, 4th edn, London, Clive Bingley, 1987, Ch.3.

4   Higginbottom, *op. cit.*

5   John Fielden Consultancy, *Fielden report.*

6   Jordan, P. with Jones, N., *Staff management in library and information work*, 3rd edn, Aldershot, Gower, 1995, Ch.7.

7   Green, L. and Clarke, R., 'Professional excellence – different views', *Library Association record*, **97** (3), March 1995, 161–2.

8   Veaner, A. B., *Academic librarianship in a transformational age: program, politics and personnel*, Boston (Mass), G. K. Hall, 1990, Ch.11.

9   Adair, J., *Effective teambuilding*, London, Pan, 1986, Chs.9 and 10.

10 Bluck, R., 'Team management and academic libraries: a case study at the University of Northumbria', *British journal of academic librarianship*, **9** (3), 1994, 224–42.

11 Conyers, A., 'Staff training and effectiveness'. In Revill, D. (ed.), *Personnel management in polytechnic libraries*, Aldershot, Gower, 1987, 53–75.

9

Staff Development for Heads of Service/Chief Librarians:
The Pilot, the Doctor and the Magician

PATRICK NOON

Introduction

When you finally drag yourself away from the fascinating world of the network navigator and a future, technologically uncertain, but full of potentially exciting cyber-bells and superhighway whistles and after you have welcomed the recognition of the chronic space problems besetting all academic libraries, you eventually get to the bit of the Follett Report[1] that talks about people. In particular, you get to the part that talks about the development needs of library staff including senior managers. You could be excused for missing it, however, because it is not very long and really does no more than refer you to another report produced by the John Fielden Consultancy.[2] Indeed, in the aftermath of Follett, all the discussions, welcome as they are, have been about money for more space, electronic libraries and retrospective conversion. With a couple of honourable exceptions there does not appear to be any enthusiasm for pursuing the staff development dimension subcontracted to Fielden, prompting more than one exasperated commentator to query why staff have not received the same fulsome support as the bells and whistles. This should not be all that surprising. Despite its prominence on publication and in the years that followed, it is a fruitless task to search the Parry Report[3] for any reasonable mention of staff development for anyone, let alone senior managers. A nod in that direction 25 years later can probably be seen as a major step forward, even if it is then subtly forgotten in high places. It is just another example of the 'British Disease': the wilful and deliberate refusal to recognize that an effective economy and effective organizations rely on adequate, continuing investment in the development of the human resources on whom their success ultimately depends. The plea by Peters and Waterman[4] – 'treat (people) not capital spending and automation as the primary source of productivity gains . If you want productivity you must treat workers as your most important asset' – continues to fall on the kind of unreceptive ears that seem more attracted to the view that 'Training a worker means merely enabling him(sic) to carry out the directions of his work schedule. Once he can do this the training is over whatever his age'.

The relevance of all of this for staff development for senior library managers is that the curious death of the human resources dimension of Follett suggests the continuing existence of opinions closer to the second view than the first. This was the view of Frank Gilbreth[5] the associate and advocate of F. W. Taylor and his supposedly discredited views on scientific management, expressed many decades ago.

In many respects this is, of course, not the case. Staff development in academic libraries has a record of which the sector can be reasonably proud. Programmes offered by the Library Association and complemented by other providers have found a ready market in academic libraries. To this can be added an impressive array of other development activities including the use of training consultants, regional cooperatives and a stimulating range of in-house initiatives to develop staff at almost all levels, in often original and cost effective ways. Almost all levels, but not quite. The curious omission is at the senior level. Here the poverty of provision seems to suggest that the view expressed by one prominent member of the profession that 'you're already a University Librarian, you don't need any development' is a widely endorsed opinion. It is not an uncommon view about senior management positions as Charles Handy[6] and his research team found when they investigated the training and development of managers in the late 80s and compared it with that of other countries. They concluded that for the British manager, common sense, character and background were more important than formal management training and education, and that experience was considered the only way to learn how to manage.

Unless we address the issue of investment in the development of staff at all levels, the sector may find itself with the senior librarians it deserves, rather than those that organizations, the profession and most importantly library staff and users need.

Development needs

The problem, though, is what are the development needs of senior library staff and how do we identify them? Maurice Line and Keith Robertson[7] offer at least one vision of why this has not been perceived as a problem in the past:

> Many librarians – most until a few years ago – were recruited as intelligent and well educated individuals who liked books, who had a good sense of social service and were interested in organising knowledge for the benefit of students or the public. They were not recruited as managers; aptitude for managing was not sought.

It is a situation that some practising University Librarians recognize well. Stuart James[8] suggests that management

> . . . crept up on many of us, but the actual realization can come quite suddenly; there we were quietly and diligently pursuing our librarianship careers when we suddenly realized we had become managers.

In circumstances where most University and College Librarians are happy to acknowledge the importance of staff development, and to offer it their support, there still seems a curious gap where staff development for those University and College Librarians, themselves, should be. As Pascale and Athos[9] pointed out some time ago, it is a question of perception:

> Management is the problem and more effective management is pivotal to improving our lot . . . We face a tough task in changing how we manage because we (managers) are a large part of the problem. We must change what we are as well as what we do.

There seem to be at least two key imperatives that dictate the desirability of a more effective approach to the development needs of senior library managers. The first is the changing nature of what senior managers are expected to do. This is driven by the second which is the dynamic nature of the environment in which those senior librarians are expected to operate.

There have been enough words written about the dynamic nature of the current environment of higher education and libraries to rival the output of Marx, and there has been enough evidence over the past decade to safely assume that Peter Drucker[10] was quite right when he asserted that

> . . . if one thing is certain it is that job requirements and organizational structure will change in the future as they have always done in the past. What is needed is the development of managers equal to the tasks of tomorrow, not the tasks of yesterday.

In a world of increasing complexity for libraries and librarians the concept that we can simply inherit a position of University or College Librarian and assume that we have the ready made skills is untenable. An illustration of this is a story told by David Clutterbuck,[11] one of the country's foremost mentoring gurus. During his early working life he was constantly amazed at what he considered poor decisions made by his manager, decisions that led Clutterbuck to conclude that the manager was, to use his phrase, 'a bit of a prat'. It was only when Clutterbuck attained that managerial position himself that he realized the complex framework within which that manager had been working, helping him make sense of what had seemed poor decisions. Within that complex framework, the decisions suddenly became a lot more comprehensible.

Role of the senior manager

If we accept the reality of this complex and dynamic context within which the senior manager has to operate, what are the implications for the role of the University or College Librarian? How must the role evolve to succeed in this environment, and what are the development implications for this changing role?

Thompson and Carr[12] provide one starting point with their definition of the role of the University Librarian

> . . . a great administrative responsibility, a large building, a considerable number of staff, a sizeable budget, a complex system of technical and professional routines, and the whole university to serve.

Whilst this might be accurate, and a bit daunting, it does not really get to the heart of identifying the essence of the job from which it might be possible to deduce the kinds of skills that have to be developed to succeed in the role. As they amplify their perception of the Librarian's role they get closer by expanding the responsibilities for staffing to include, 'confessor, arbitrator, counsellor, psychiatrist', adding the building up of stock, the provision and maintenance of accommodation and equipment and elsewhere they acknowledge the need for forecasting and planning and powers of leadership. The problem recognized by Thompson and Carr is that the more senior the job the less precise and prescriptive the job description. Even if it were possible to produce a precise job description, it seems unlikely to be detailed enough to embrace the roles needed to succeed in a world where carrying on as we did before, or continuing to do what the job description says, will not be sufficient to survive. Where work is routine, and the environment static, predetermined functions are fine. When the world around us changes, so must the skills we are able to display. There is no shortage of management writers keen to offer their prescription for this condition.

Research on the role of the senior executive is neatly summarized by Charles Handy[13] in his influential book *Understanding organizations* which also offers his own ideas on the present and future for managers and organizations . As well as some functions that may be considered implicit in any senior manager's role, such as liaison, monitor, disseminator, his list has some echoes of Thompson and Carr[12] including such roles as disturbance handler, negotiator, resource allocator and leader. It also, however, includes some important additional, and far more nebulous roles such as figurehead, spokesperson and entrepreneur, the last being a role increasingly familiar in education at all levels. Charles Handy suggests that any manager's job will comprise these in differing mixes depending on the organization and the individual as well as on the organizational context. How much of each role we need to adopt will have to be determined by ourselves and will change as circumstances change. It is really only managers themselves who can define what the exact role for their context will be. It also seems reasonable to suggest that few senior librarians will come into such an unpredictable role completely equipped to fulfil all these requirements.

One of the more popular current images of the manager's job is that created by Handy himself, what he calls the helicopter factor, the ability to rise above day to day activities and take in all the wider implications of those activities, set them in their context and understand the wider vision. This is not unlike Peter Drucker's suggestion that a senior manager 'keeps his nose to the grindstone whilst lifting his eyes to the hills'. Handy identifies this as one of the managerial dilemmas that face the modern manager: time horizons, or balancing present demands with future need. University and College Librarians will be familiar with having to live in this complex world with two competing and sometimes conflicting time frames. They will recognize the struggle to keep a present inadequate library building limping along whilst planning the new one for three years time; arguing for funding for escalating journal prices whilst planning for an access rather than holdings policy for the future; keeping staff happy and motivated whilst planning new structures that will meet changing needs.

Handy's other analogy is that of the manager as general practitioner. Not simply in the role of dispenser of cures for ills, but in the other, often imperceptible, role of doctor as analyst; asking questions, probing issues, finding the real problem that contributes to the referred pain, identifying options, distinguishing cures from placebos.

Rosemary Stewart's model of the manager's work summarized by Handy does not offer pre-determined roles but instead identifies a function required to make choices, influenced, on the one hand, by the demands made upon the manager, and on the other, by the constraints limiting the freedom to make those choices.[13] The volatile nature of the constraints and demands within which the manager must work represent exactly the same kind of dynamic and unpredictable environment portrayed by Rosabeth Moss Kanter,[14] another writer keen to point the way towards new definitions of the manger's role. Acknowledging the dynamism of organizational environments, Kanter suggests that successful managers must now expect to '. . . learn to ask questions rather than assume there are pre-existing answers, to trust the process of operating in the realm of faith and hope and embryonic possibility'.

This is a very different universe from the deterministic world of Gilbreth! Above all, for Kanter and Handy, managing is about the future and about articulating a vision of that future that others can follow. Handy argues that the manager is 'above all responsible for the future' and Kanter talks about 'the deliberate and conscious articulation of a direction' and 'creating a vision of a possible future that allows them and others to see more clearly the steps to take' or about 'creating larger visions and engaging people's imagination in pursuit of them'.

To achieve these demanding expectations Kanter argues that we cannot rely solely on traditional management approaches. There is a growing realization that when the environment is unpredictable then so must be the manager's response. Intuition, innovation, entrepreneurship and imagination are increasingly the words that are used to describe the roles needed to succeed in complex circumstances. Conventional management techniques offer an invaluable tool-kit for the manager but they can˙ also stifle 'leaps of the imagination and leaps of faith' and the 'artful crafting of an image of possibilities'.

Using one of her more graphic analogies, Kanter argues that managers must be like the magician performing the well known trick with five rings. The rings that are displayed to the audience are all separate solid and unbroken at the outset but, through the extraordinary skills of the magician, the rings all end up connected within one another. No one but the magician knows how this feat has been achieved but everyone is suitably amazed by the way the impossible has become a new possibility.

The ability to diagnose situations in the full knowledge of both present and future needs and to articulate the right direction from this, the ability to rise above the immediate and see the whole picture in its context and the ability to juggle self contained and separate factors before combining them to create a unified vision and a firmly linked strategy: these are the skills of the senior manager in a complex and dynamic world. They must be entrepreneurs and leaders at the same time as coping with confessions and confusion; they must be as adept at handling disturbance as they are at controlling resources. They need imagination, and new approaches to conventional thinking to help overcome suffocating constraints and to make the most of the myriad possibilities that complex worlds have to offer. It seems logical, then, that these too are the skills of the University or College Librarian facing the kind of environment articulated by the Follett Report and all too familiar to anyone currently working in the sector. Lynne Brindley,[15] talking long before Follett brought much of this into sharp focus argued, like Kanter, that we can no longer rely on doing the same old things because they worked last time. She pictured a future

> in which adaptability and flexibility are the key. We will need to be able to cope positively with continuing change, to create our own opportunities, fre-

quently without precedence to guide us, and develop the capacity to deal with increasing complexity of choice and decision making.

That future is now all too clearly our present and the kinds of tactical, strategic and political skills alluded to here are not necessarily those that the University or College Librarian, was born with, has acquired or sometimes even recognizes as the skills that may have made the position attractive in the first place. Brindley continues by pointing out the tools that we need to acquire and develop if we are to succeed:

> . . . a positive attitude to planning with associated management science techniques . . . is . . . an essential part of the management kitbag for the information professional of the future. The increasingly complex environment requires us to develop the ability to ask better quality questions and use quantified information more systematically in answering them.

Even for those who have acquired some or many of these management skills the learning and development process must still continue if they are to cope successfully with the dramatically changed imperatives within which education is now forced to operate. With some prescience Brindley recognizes this too when she warns that

> . . . innovation will not come without pain and conflict for which we as managers need better preparation, particularly as many of us have been trained and developed managerially over a period when it was thought preferable to smooth over problems rather than tackle them head on.

The kinds of changes that education continues to suffer will inevitably lead all senior managers to have to make increasingly difficult or imaginative decisions about people, resources and collections. Finding strategies for coping with all this both personally and organizationally ought to be an important development issue.

Development and the future

In the aftermath of Follett and Fielden the first question that has to be addressed is do the University or College Librarians of today and tomorrow have the kinds of skills that seem to be necessary to succeed in the complex and dynamic world of education? Neither Follett nor Fielden appear convinced that they do. Follett warns librarians not to allow their professional identity to isolate them from institutional management, suggesting that this is exactly the situation that exists in some institutions, presumably to the detriment of both the senior manager and the library service. The report reinforces this view with the criticism that training for managers has been given inadequate attention by many libraries. Fielden comments that the provision of management development across the sector is inadequate and needs to be enhanced. If the answer to the first question is that senior managers do not all have all the skills necessary to deliver successful library services, the second question must be how can we develop those skills? This presumes an affirmative answer to the unasked question 'Do senior managers wish to develop these skills?'. How we develop them may not be easy, particularly as effective management development requires some searching and fundamental questions, of the kind suggested by Drucker.

> What organisation will be needed to attain the objectives of tomorrow? What management jobs will that require? What qualifications will managers have to have to be equal to the demands of tomorrow? What additional skills will they have to acquire, what knowledge, what abilities will they have to possess?[10]

What can only be described as a full scale management development industry has grown up to attempt to answer these questions, which are just as relevant to University and College Librarians as they are to anyone in industry or other areas of public service. Peter Drucker suggests that this particular service industry is absolutely crucial to the concept of successful management. He argues that it is the way we make work more than just a way of earning a living, so there ought to be no shortage of solutions to the issue of development for senior staff. Those solutions will, however, only ever be of any use if we are able, successfully, to identify the problem. The first part of the problem is to recognize the need for a properly structured approach to development for senior staff that continues throughout professional life rather than being accomplished early as a foundation for future greatness. Amongst the staffing projections in *Information UK 2000*[16] was a recognition that the expectation that we should get all of our learning and training done at one go will be outmoded. There is also the prediction of an increasingly blurred division between initial learning and continuing professional development as librarians and information workers develop the range of political, financial and personnel skills necessary for senior posts. In Handy's words, 'our stock of learning and conditioning will need continual replenishment'.

The growing acceptance that this kind of continuing development is the key to future success is still, sadly, inhibited by the misapprehension that development is something that is done to staff and, from a senior manager's perspective, done to other people. Mumford's research[17] found that support for organizational development schemes was accompanied, at the highest levels, by a widespread failure to take part in those schemes. This is a manifestation of what Mumford refers to as the management development paradox; the belief amongst many practising managers that they can learn management best from their own experience rather than from any other external agency or facilitation, despite clear evidence that managers, particularly in Britain, lack the skills and knowledge to manage effectively. Handy and his fellow researchers found another aspect of the same phenomenon; the curious belief that the British manager is just born with the necessary skills.

> It is strange that . . . unlike almost any other important job or position there is no proficiency test for would be managers, no required training, no apprenticeship. The drivers of our organisations do not even need 'L' plates let alone a licence. Management it seems is something that most people are expected to be able to do, like parenting, picking it up as you go along . . . other countries do not believe that so important a job can be left to so accidental a process.

The conclusions in the Follett and Fielden Reports suggest that academic libraries may be equally guilty of these convenient self deceptions.

Routes to development

The second part of the problem is to address any development needs in the most appropriate way, a situation made more difficult by the persistent, and misguided, assumption that development means 'going on courses'. In certain circumstances, but not all, formal development such as a course offers a convenient and neatly packaged approach, and there are valuable examples of the kinds of courses that could produce just the kind of change in attitudes towards managing academic libraries urged by Follett and Fielden. Most Departments of Library and Information Studies offer higher degrees or in-service programmes that can provide a great deal of the formal management background that some University and College

Librarians may feel they lack. Broader, if potentially more challenging approaches are offered by the myriad MBAs now available, including at least one focusing specifically on the information sector. Less intellectual but just as valuable, virtually any Management School in the country offers a bewildering array of postgraduate certificates and diplomas providing a practical approach to the issues and dilemmas of management. Many of these programmes, following the lead offered by the Management Charter Initiative are adopting a competences-based approach to management development, laying great emphasis on workplace experience and trying to weld together the academic dimension with the natural belief that even without any formal training, not all managers can have been getting it all wrong all the time! This has very much been the approach adopted by the two attempts within the library sector to develop a strategic management skills programme for senior managers. The initial pilot programmes run for the British Library hoped to produce a 'highly skilled management capable of matching the best professional managers . . . to fill our most senior management positions'[18] and were successful up to the point where the real cost had to be faced. The SCONUL version based on a recognized Business School offered a highly successful development of this approach. Balancing a substantial financial investment with leading edge management development, *Managing for success*, as it was called, received considerable endorsement from its initial cohort. Such programmes will never be a complete answer to the development needs of senior library managers but they have the potential to make a very valuable contribution provided that librarians are prepared to embrace the proposition that such development is not only desirable but, increasingly, vital.

Virtually every commentator on management development, however, is quick to point out that courses and qualifications, for all their efficiency and ubiquity, are only a very small part of the development process. They are happy to agree with those still sceptical about the management development process that at senior levels formal development has its limitations. Where these commentators would depart from the sceptics, though, is by asserting that the void should not be filled with the usual reliance on common sense or seat of the pants approaches so often passed off as experience. Personal experience is absolutely vital to the development of managers and librarians alike, but as Handy points out 'experience has to be reflected upon, understood and subsequently improved if there is to be any true learning beyond the crude "I won't do that again"'.

As well as courses there has always been a variety of alternative and often far more challenging vehicles for delivering this kind of reflection, and thereby, the development upon which effective management relies.

The current resurgence of interest in topics such as mentoring is a useful example of the highly personalized alternative to off-the-shelf programmes, where experience and development can be reflected upon with the help and support of someone happy to take on the role of personal developer, champion or coach. The idea of more experienced colleagues taking on a one-to-one development, counselling or coaching role with a less experienced colleague, to enable the one to learn from the experience of the other is as old as the oldest crafts but in its intellectual guise is increasingly being seen as a powerful development tool for those willing and able to recognize the potential. Higher education, with long standing, and well established, network organizations such as SCONUL and the Higher Education Colleges Learning Resources Group (HCLRG), ought to have no trouble in establishing a framework within which such relationships can be promoted. This should be particularly true now, in the light of the British Library-funded research being undertaken into mentoring in the library and information profession by the Library Association's Personnel Training and Education Group and the Department of Library and Information Studies at the University of Central England.

A variation on this kind of shared development activity has indeed, already been tried informally by SCONUL. The so-called Class of 86, a group of new University Librarians who took up their posts in or around 1986, met on a number of occasions to share experiences, build networks and look for a practical alternative to formal development activities. A repeat version based on new incumbents from a couple of years later attempted to share the experience of the older group. Out of what were recognized as valuable experiences grew a similar network of University Deputy Librarians from SCONUL and a similar group based on a COPOL version of the same idea, before these two organizations amalgamated. The two deputies groups and the Class of '86 continue to prosper suggesting that all of them offer important models of how valuable this kind of informal self help approach to development can be; a model that could perhaps have much wider application.

In a chapter of this length it is not possible to offer detailed insights into other examples of informal development vehicles. Besides, it has been much more effectively done by Alan Mumford, whose book *Management development: strategies for action*[17] provides an invaluable overview of the potential for development, both in and off the job. Counselling, coaching, more details of mentoring, as well as action learning are all introduced. The latter offers a more formal version of the Class of '86, where specific learning experiences can be shared by a group of mutually supportive peers. Individual development grows out of those experiences and the group reflection upon them. As if to corroborate this approach Handy and his colleagues suggest a similar array of opportunities based on the Japanese approach 'a learning culture with a battery of devices . . . planned job rotation, mentors, group discussions, study visits . . . book courses and the constant search for the better way'.

SCONUL and HCRLG either together or individually could of course provide the vehicle for any or all of these approaches to development for the senior librarians whom they represent. Indeed the Fielden Report charges them with such a responsibility and SCONUL even has a Staffing Advisory Committee through whom these approaches could be channelled. That, however, would be to miss one of the most important dimensions of the whole question of development for such senior staff; that individuals themselves must recognize, and be prepared to take action to meet, their development needs.

The survey conducted on behalf of the Follett Committee found that there were indeed some development needs identified by senior managers. There was, however, not much of a mention of the need to develop the basic tools of management. Nor, it would appear, of the need to understand complex environments or to understand how to manage in a world where uncertainty and unpredictability are likely to be the only constant factors. There is a danger that unless individuals analyse their development needs in a properly structured way they simply focus on whatever is new, believing that we are all already able managers because we have been there and done that, oblivious to the trail of havoc left behind by a combination of poor communication, lack of vision and non-existent strategy. Perhaps the comparative dearth of appropriate development activities for University and College Librarians is because of an understandable, but self-defeating desire to avoid an admission of the need for self development. As most commentators agree, the responsibility for replenishing skills and knowledge will increasingly, and quite rightly, belong to the individual no matter how senior. Line managers can help, peers can contribute and staff can provide clues but at senior levels development, like fleshing out the vague job description, is a very personal responsibility. This may, of course, be one reason why there is not the recognition that perhaps there ought to be about the importance of development at the highest levels. To take self development seriously requires some difficult and searching self analysis of ourselves and our needs, and as Charles Handy points out this is not something we are very comfortable with: 'we have to face realities we had hoped to ignore'. It is still surprisingly difficult to persuade people that a recognition of a need to develop is not an admission of weakness but an important and badly neglected strength.

Finally, if self awareness and recognition of development needs can be achieved it only leaves one familiar barrier to be overcome; finding the time. Some University and College Librarians are far from alone in nobly foregoing opportunities for personal and professional development, arguing that at their level they simply cannot afford to spend the time on such self referential indulgences no matter how much they might claim to recognize the need and, besides, someone else would be denied a development opportunity. In a world where change is constant and in the context in which the University and College Librarian's work is becoming more dynamic than anyone can be comfortable with, it is more likely that they cannot afford not to find the time to spend on their own development – particularly if this is likely to embrace helicopter pilot lessons, working on their GP's bedside manner or joining the Magic Circle.

References

1   *Follett report.*
2   *Fielden report.*
3   *Report of the Committee on Libraries*, University grants committee, London, London, 1967.
4   Peters T. and Waterman R., *In search of excellence*, London, Harper Row, 1982.
5   Gilbreth, F., Quoted in Braverman H., *Labour and monopoly capitalism*, New York, Monthly Review Press, 1974.
6   Handy, C. Gordon, C. Gow I. and Randlesome, C., *Making managers*, London, Pitman, 1988.
7   Line, M. and Robertson K., 'Staff development in libraries', *British journal of academic librarianship*, **4** (3), 1989, 161–76.
8   James, S. 'The manager and the library: a review of some general and industrial management books and their relevance to library management', *Librarian career development*, **2** (2), 1994, 18–22.
9   Pascale, R. T. and Athos, A. G., *The art of Japanese management*, London, Allen Lane, 1982.
10 Drucker, P., *The practice of management*, Oxford, Butterworth-Heinmann, 1993.
11 Goldsmith, W. and Clutterbuck, D., *The winning streak*, Harmondsworth, Penguin, 1985.
12 Thompson, J. and Carr, R , *An introduction to university library administration*, 4th edn, London, Bingley, 1987.
13 Handy, C., *Understanding organizations*, London, Penguin, 1993.
14 Kanter, R. M., *The change masters*, 4th edn, London, Unwin, 1985.
15 Brindley, L., 'Management development for the information professionals of the future', *Aslib proceedings*, **39** (9), 1987, 235–43.
16 Martyn, J., Vickers, P. and Feeney, M., *Information UK 2000*, London, Bowker-Saur, 1990.
17 Mumford, A., *Management development: strategies for action*, 2nd edn, London, IPM, 1993.
18 Malley, I., 'Cash is the key for management training', *Library Association record*, **94** (12), 1992.

10

Human Resource Development in Academic and Research Libraries: an American perspective

SUSAN JUROW

Introduction

Depending on personal experience and workplace philosophy, terms like 'training', 'staff development', and 'continuing education' have a wide variety of meanings. To clarify the frame within which this chapter offers comments, I would like to provide the following definition of 'human resource development' written by Leonard Nadler,[1] a well-known American professor of adult education and human resource development:

> ... human resource development is the activity of an organization that provides organized learning experiences for a specified period of time for the possibility of improving job performance or the growth of employees.

The three key points within this definition are the focus on learning, the need to allocate discrete blocks of time for this activity, and the critical role of the organization in turning the possibility of learning into a reality. Dr Nadler goes on to emphasize that the main purpose of human resource development is improved job performance. He identifies three areas of activity: training (job-related with a problem-solving orientation), education (preparation for a future position), and development (directed at personal growth).

A recent US Department of Education document helps to clarify the scope of these three areas further: training is assistance in maintaining professional knowledge and skills; education is preparation for assuming new responsibilities or changing career paths; and development is a broadening of the practitioner's knowledge and skills to cope with new developments and achieve flexibility in complex work environments.[2]

Some may see human resource development as a very broad mandate for academic and research libraries, especially during periods of financial constraint. I would argue that, for reasons unique to the academic environment and because of attitudes prevalent today in the broader world of business and industry, this is the direction toward which these institutions are and have been moving for over 20 years. It is also the only viable direction if academic and research libraries are to remain central to the teaching and research missions of their host institutions.

The past

As early as 1981, most large academic and research libraries in the United States had professional and staff training and development programmes that included general orientation; skills training provided on a departmental basis; and special focus workshops dealing with organizational, interpersonal, and personal issues such as conducting surveys, managing conflict, and stress management. Responsibility rested largely with the personnel librarian with some involvement of committees to plan, assess, and serve as a clearing-house.[3]

A review of the US library literature to update this picture reveals that little has been written on the topic of human resource development in the past five years. The focus of the few articles that have appeared is primarily on training as previously defined, e.g. training for reference, for collection development, and more recently, for customer service and for teaching Internet skills to the public. The articles with a development focus dealt most often with learning to handle constant change, especially in the area of technology.

The contemporary training, education, and development issues of concern to library professionals charged with responsibility for human resource development are reflected in a 1991 discussion of the Association of College and Research Libraries (ACRL) Personnel and Staff Development Officers Discussion Group. Their programme addressed the variety of ways training takes place and roles of the parties involved, from senior management to the individual engaged in the learning experience. The value of performance appraisals as a learning tool, funding, and training by vendors were discussed, as was the problem of plateaued staff.[4]

Responsibility

Responsibility for human resource development in academic and research libraries resides with a number of individuals and institutions. It rests with the employee, their supervisor, the institution where they are employed, and the profession at large, including library schools' responsibility to provide continuing education opportunities, and library associations that represent member needs. This applies equally to librarians and library staff.

In the United States, library associations play an important role in the provision of human resource development opportunities. The American Library Association (ALA) uses its biannual meetings to offer a wide array of programmes on topics selected by members through the standing committee structure.

The subgroups within ALA, such as ACRL, the Library Administration and Management Association (LAMA), and the Library and Information Technology Association (LITA) all sponsor conferences, workshops, and short courses that build technical expertise and have particular relevance for academic librarians. In 1992, LAMA published the second edition of a how-to manual on creating a staff development programme that was prepared by the Staff Development Committee of the Personnel Administration Section.[5]

The Special Library Association (SLA) focuses primarily on the needs of those who work in corporate, government, and specialized library environments. Some academic librarians, especially those who work in libraries with a business or science focus, take advantage of SLA's programming. The Medical Library Association (MLA) has a sophisticated and highly regarded continuing education programme. The American Association of Law Librarians (AALL) relies heavily on its own members to offer training programmes selected and developed by working committees. The Council on Library/Media Technicians (COLT) has become increasingly active in promoting and sponsoring training, education, and development programmes for library staff.

The Association of Research Libraries (ARL) which represents the 119 largest academic and research libraries in the United States and Canada has had a programme devoted to organizational and staff development since 1970, the Office of Management Services (OMS). Offering management consulting, management training, and management information services, the OMS reaches over 1,000 library staff and professionals each year through workshops offered publicly or sponsored by individual institutions. Over the past ten years, demand for these workshops has grown from four public and two sponsored institutes per year to six public and 15 sponsored institutes per year. A sharp increase over the past three years in the number of workshops sponsored by individual or regional groups of libraries reflects the decrease in funding for travel for development purposes.

Some library and information science programmes have integrated continuing education into their curricula to a greater degree than others. For example, the University of California at Berkeley and the University of Michigan have certificate programmes that offer librarians the opportunity to develop a depth of expertise after receiving their MLS degree in areas such as bibliography, library automation, library management, and information management.

Funding

According to the American Society for Training and Development (ASTD), industry spends on average 1.4% of payroll on training. Two percent is the minimum recommended by ASTD.[6] A recent survey of the Urban Library Council (ULC) found that 60% of their members spent less than 1% of their personnel budgets on staff development. The need to 'keep the branches open' was blamed for the low levels of funding. '. . . an institution undergoing radical changes that is not retraining workers to cope with those changes . . .' was the serious consequence identified by Joey Rodgers, ULC Executive Director.[7]

Some libraries have been able to raise human resource development funds from sources outside their institutional budgets, including private funds and grants. One source has been the Friends of the Library, ad hoc organizations affiliated with many US libraries that assist with fundraising activities. Some library directors have chosen to use gift funds that have not been targeted for other uses by donors.

The H. W. Wilson Company, which produces many of the bibliographic indexes used in libraries, established a library staff development fund, administered through the American Library Association. The $2,500 competitive award is offered annually to the library organization that can document and demonstrate commitment and ability to implement a staff development programme. It has been awarded to programmes as diverse as developing interpersonal skills to upgrading the technical skills of interlibrary loan staff.

Some of the large state university systems, such as the University of California, have system-wide funds available for programmes that encourage participation from multiple campuses. The faculty union of the State University of New York (SUNY) system has been successful in the past in negotiating for training and development funding as part of their union contract.

One of the issues sometimes raised in funding discussions is the degree to which individuals should take financial responsibility for their own training and development. A recent research study found that institutional support correlates positively with professional activities.[8] Institutional support was defined both as release time and as financial assistance. If support was offered for attendance at professional meetings, librarians were more active professionally; if support was offered for continuing education, librarians attended more workshops; if support was offered for research, librarians published more, applied for and received more grants; and if support was offered for taking credit courses, more librarians took part in degree-granting programs. Each institution must assess the degree to which it can afford to support financially the behaviour it would like exhibited by staff.

Programming

The library literature of the past five years provides a number of interesting examples of locally-designed programmes that offer innovative approaches to training, education, and development of librarians and library staff.

Training

Developing reference skills is an old problem with a number of contemporary twists. Besides the traditional concerns of building the skills of new librarians and of staying current with new reference sources, the reference department in many large academic and research libraries must seek help from support staff and librarians in other fields to cover the range of services now being offered.[9] Providing a firm foundation with a well-designed orientation programme is one approach.[10] Coaching by a peer/mentor has been used to extend and enhance traditional training programmes.[11, 12]

A relatively new challenge is keeping technology skills up to date in a rapidly expanding arena. Librarians and library staff must keep current with changes in their local systems, commercial bibliographic search systems, the Internet, the World Wide Web, as well as CD-ROM systems. While vendors may provide some of the training support for new systems, locally-developed programmes also provide opportunities for building in-house training skills based on adult learning theory.[13]

Education

Most of the programmes designed to prepare individuals to assume new responsibilities focus on the development of managers. One of the best known programmes is run by the Council on Library Resources (CLR). For almost 20 years, the CLR Academic Library Management Intern Program has placed senior academic library middle managers in libraries for a one-year period to work closely with the director and senior administrative staff to '. . . observe and participate in management activities and undertake special assignments. The goal of the program is to expose interns to the complete array of policy matters and operating problems of a large research library.'[14]

A number of universities, e.g. Stanford University and the University of Chicago, have created programmes for experienced middle managers to learn more about the administration of the university and to build a network of colleagues; librarians have been invited to participate in these programmes for a number of years. They consist of regular meetings held around the campus with a variety of senior university administrators and provide an opportunity for the larger organizations to assess the skills of valued employees and extend their career opportunities.

A variation on this approach was developed in the Chicago area between the libraries of Northwestern University, the University of Illinois at Chicago Circle, and the University of Chicago.[15] This programme, which consists of a series of seminars offered on the three campuses, provides opportunities for librarians new to academic librarianship to understand the complexities of three large and distinct research institutions. As with other similar programmes, one of the peripheral benefits is the network of colleagues that is built during such an experience.

Development

Today's complex environment has spawned a host of issues unique to this era that require a new level of 'coping' ability on the part of library staff and professionals. They include problems such as 'technostress' and dealing with constant change. They also include new ways of operating in the workplace such as developing an appreciation and support for diversity, and working in teams.

The problem of plateaued staff, i.e. staff who stop operating at peak performance because of a perceived lack of stimulation and/or reward, has been perceived as relatively common in academic and research libraries where the tenure of both professional and support staff is long. It is a problem, in part, specific to the Baby Boom Generation reaching a period when those striving for upper management are stopped by the limited number of positions, a number growing even smaller as library organizations downsize and de-layer management. It is also a problem that is exacerbated during periods of economic constraint when jobs are scarce and mobility limited.

Libraries have used a variety of approaches to this problem, including internal transfers that enhance skill base, cross-training that increases the scope of responsibility, and projects that provide opportunities for personal accomplishment and contribution. Seeking challenging work that fits individual needs is a joint responsibility of the manager and the employee. The manager must have the resources to offer opportunities and training to engage new situations, and the employee must recognize the need and have the desire to broaden his or her knowledge and skills. The key is recognition that personal growth is still an option when vertical mobility is not.[16]

The librarians in 30% of the libraries that belong to ARL have faculty status or its equivalent on their campus. They share with the teaching and research faculty the benefit of sabbaticals, which can be especially useful in refreshing, retooling, and renewal.[17]

Local practice

In preparation for a large-scale inquiry into approaches to and support for training and staff development, ARL recently surveyed its members through the OMS Systems and Procedures Exchange Center (SPEC). The survey requested information about library policies and plans for training and staff development, and the locus of responsibility and budgeting for these programmes. Approximately 40% of the Association's 108 academic library members responded, some offering background documents to illustrate their approaches. The responses provide a snapshot of human resource development trends within the academic and research library community and insight into a variety of local practices.

Policy

The policy statement is where the organization confirms its commitment to training and to the principles underlying support for staff development. It defines the variety of terms associated with these issues and clarifies what activities fall within the local definitions. Staffing and funding are generally addressed as well. Just over one third of respondents said that their institutions had developed or were in the process of developing a library policy on training and staff development.

Plan

About a third of the institutions responding to the survey reported having a training and staff development plan. The plans included goals and objectives, and priorities for the programme. At Dartmouth College Library, the start-up year priorities included preparing an inventory of existing programmes in the library and on campus, conducting a needs assessment, identifying resources to meet needs, and documenting activities and progress.[18]

Some plans relate the training and staff development programme directly to library performance objectives. The University of California at San Diego Libraries plan offers the following example:

> Shared Decision Making: provide staff development training in support of Shared Decision Making for staff to develop expertise in areas of team building, communication, conflict management, facilitation, and group process, so

that they may successfully carry out the goals and objectives of their Department and the Organization.[19]

Responsibility

A number of the policy statements designate library administration and supervisors as carrying primary responsibility for staff development. It is acknowledged, however, that it is a responsibility shared with the individual employee.

In about one third of the institutions the (library) personnel officer was responsible for the training and staff development programme. The rest of the libraries were divided evenly between having a training/staff development officer, using a training/staff development committee, and joint responsibility held by the personnel officer with the assistance of a training and staff development committee. A small number of institutions reported that the responsibility for training and staff development rested at the departmental level.

Training and staff development committees are generally broadly-based in membership, including both librarians and support staff. They are generally responsible for acting as a clearinghouse for local and off-site training opportunities, and for developing in-house programmes, such as brown bag lunch discussions, film series, and guest lectures. Depending on the interest, energy, and expertise of the committee, this is sometimes based on an interest or needs survey of library staff.

At one institution where recent organizational development initiatives have resulted in a more team-based organization, a 'Learning Team' has been created to integrate the principles of the 'learning organization' more deeply into the organization.

Budget

Budgets varied in size from no separately allocated funds to a budget in excess of $100,000. About 10% of the respondents stated that no separate budget line existed, often adding that requests were approved individually or that the size of the budget was dependent upon what was being offered in that year. Approximately half of the respondents reported budgets in the $5,000 to $20,000 range, and a quarter reported budgets in the $20,000 to $45,000 range. The remaining organizations reported budgets over $55,000.

The budgets were seldom broken down by type of staff, e.g. librarians or support staff. In the few cases where separate budgets did exist, another budget line was also designated either for library-wide programming or for 'official' business. In one case, $40,000 was allocated directly to each of six department heads. It was not possible to discern how many or which institutions separated funding for the programmes from funding for the travel to the programmes.

In one case, the guidelines for the allocation of resources for training and staff development are contained within the continuing education policy. They state that one quarter of the available budgeted amount will be spent on local or in-house sessions, one quarter will be spent on attendance at programs off-site, and half for attendance at the conferences of professional bodies.

Programming

When comparing the current training and staff development programming of these institutions with the training and staff development programme calendars of the past, the most obvious difference is in the number and variety of workshops related to technology. In the 1970s and early 1980s, workshops on online searching and local systems first appeared. In the 1980s, training programmes for software packages were added. In the 1990s, workshops on using local email systems, the Internet, and the World Wide Web have become more prevalent. Most recently, workshops on tagging protocols such as SGML and HTML are being offered.

Examples of typical current training, education, and development programmes can be gleaned from a review of published training schedules. Some of the newer training programmes relate to customer service and grow out of the Total Quality Management (TQM) or continuous improvement movement. They include workshops on topics such as dealing with angry customers on the phone, and designing needs assessments or customer satisfaction surveys.

Most of the in-house education programmes relate to management skills and could also be characterized as training, depending on whether the individual involved currently holds a management position or aspires to one. Programmes on goal setting, motivating staff, and performance evaluation fall into this category. As the staff size of many of these libraries has been reduced, responsibility for the duties

that have traditionally belonged under public services, like bibliographic instruction, are being shared with library staff from other
parts of the library, requiring programmes on development of hand-
outs and teaching strategies.

In the arena of development, training in coping skills has been part
of the programming for the past 20 years, including time and stress
management workshops. Workshops on managing change have been
added to this repertoire. An understanding of workplace ergonomics
has become increasingly important as cases of carpal tunnel syn-
drome and other repetitive motion injuries related to computer use
become more prevalent.

A fairly recent and growing entry is diversity training, leading to
an understanding of and appreciation for human differences found
in the workplace. This programming reflects the rapidly changing
demographics taking place in the United States with larger numbers
of minorities entering the workforce and as academic and research
library users. These programmes are often university mandated.

The future

If academic and research libraries are to be successful players in the
world of constant inexorable change which we anticipate, the future
of training, education, and development in the workplace will have
to be something called the 'learning organization,' a term most often
identified with Peter Senge, author of *The fifth discipline*. A learning
organization is a place '. . . where people continually expand their
capabilities to understand complexity, clarify vision, and improve
shared mental models that is, they are responsible for learning'.[20]
Proponents of this concept argue that it is the only way organizations
will be able to build the flexibility and fluidity of practice needed
constantly to shift priorities, to reinvent roles, and to build new skills
together, as a cohesive entity.

In the United States, some library managers and administrators
are beginning to articulate what this would mean. Susan Lee,[21]
Associate Librarian of Harvard College for Administration, envisages a central training department where

Staff development and training will be for organizational and system
renewal and effectiveness' and that 'Rather than as experts and teachers, the
trainers will see themselves as consultants and change agents.'[1]

Shelley Phipps,[22] Assistant University Librarian at the University of Arizona writes

> We have an incredible reservoir of creative, energetic talent in our academic research libraries . . . This leaves great room for new and creative ways of thinking about what librarianship is all about and transforming libraries to serve the ultimate cause of learning.[22]

Shifting our understanding of human resource development from training and education to learning is our greatest challenge. Each individual, whether library leader, librarian, or library staff, will need to take personal responsibility for building personal and organizational competence. Academic libraries, like the corporate sector, will have to make a greater investment in human resource development because to be successful, we will have constantly to reinvent our programmes and services to meet the evolving needs, skills, and goals of our clients. To do that, we will have constantly to be reinventing ourselves.

References

1 Nadler,L. J., 'HRD in perspective'. In Tracey, W. R., *Human resources management and development handbook*, New York, AMACOM, 1985, 13.
2 Hunt, E. S. (ed.), *Professional workers as learners: the scope, problems and accountability of continuing professional education in the 1990s*, Washington, DC, US Dept. of Education, 1992.
3 *Staff development*, Flyer no. 75, Washington, DC, Association of Research Libraries Office of Management Services and Procedures Exchange Centre, 1981.
4 'ACRL discussion group addresses staff development,' *Library personnel news*, 5 (3), 1991, 6–7
5 Lipow, A. G. and Carver, D. A., *Staff development: a practical guide*, Chicago, ALA, 1992.
6 Jurow, S. and Webster, D. E., 'Promoting management excellence in research libraries through training and staff development,' *Library administration and management*, 4 (3), 1990, 142.
7 'ULC study finds libraries invest little in staff development,' *Library journal*, 118, 1993, 112.
8 Havener, W. M. and Stolt, W., 'Professional activities of academic librarians: does institutional support make a difference?,' *College and research libraries*, 55, 1994, 25–36.
9 Glascoff, A. and Morrow, L., 'Training technical services staff to provide public services', *Illinois libraries*, 72 (8), 1990, 611–13.
10 Wogaman, M. L., 'Training newly-appointed reference librarians,' *College and research libraries news*, Jan. 1992, 9.

11   Authur, G., 'Peer coaching in a university reference department,' *College and research libraries*, **51**, 1990, 367–73.

12   Nofsinger, M. M. and Lee, A. S. W., 'Beyond orientation: the roles of senior librarians in the training of entry-level reference colleagues,' *College and research libraries*, **55**, 1994, 63–70.

13   Epple, M., Gardner, J. and Warwick R. T., 'Staff training and automated systems: 20 tips for success,' *Journal of academic librarianship*, **18** (2), 1992, 87–9.

14   Council on Library Resources, Inc., *Thirty-fifth annual report*, CLR, Washington, DC, 1992, 12.

15   Grumling, D. K. and Sheeny, C. A., 'Professional development program: training for success wihtin academic librarianship,' *College and research libraries*, **54**, 1993, 17–24.

16   DeLon, B., 'Keeping plateaued performed motivated,' *Library personnel news*, **6** (4), 1992, 6–7.

17   Reynolds, S .J., 'Sabbatical: the pause that refreshes,' *Journal of academic librarianship*, **16** (2), 1990, 90–3.

18   *Progress report*, Staff Training and Development Committee, Dartmouth College Library, June 9, 1995.

19   'Goals and objective,' *Library training plan*, University of California at San Diego Libraries , 27 Sept., 1995.

20   Senge, P., *The fifth discipline; the art and practice of the learning organization*, New York, Doubleday, 1990, 340.

21   Lee, S., 'Organizational change in research libraries,' *Journal of library administration*, **18** (3/4), 1993, 138.

22   Phipps, S., 'Transforming libraries into learning organizations – the challenge for leadership,' *Journal of library administration*, **18** (3/4), 1993, 37.

11

The Future

Margaret Oldroyd

Introduction

The analysis of change in higher education and its environment which Professor Partington gives in Chapter 1 is echoed throughout the chapters following it which evaluate the immediate contextual factors for staff development in academic libraries. A number of the specific issues which she highlights for the sector are also seen as important areas of debate for library staff.

Roles in continuing professional development (CPD)

For example, there still exists a tension for some staff about moving from recognition of the need for continuing professional development to use of the Library Association's CPD framework (which remains voluntary) or to acceptance of the role of universities, as employers, in directing their CPD. The relative roles of the professional body and the librarian, of the individual and the employer are shifting in a world where CPD needs to be obligatory for all staff.

Specific or generic needs?

Another example is the need to identify to what extent the training and development needs of library staff are genuinely specific to them and how far they have generic needs shared with other groups of university staff. Should chief librarians have a special training programme or are their needs the same as those of other senior managers? Do issue desk staff benefit most from tailor-made training or should they participate in customer care programmes for 'front-line' staff from all over the university? As universities move towards a situation where defined (accredited?) programmes of training and development are available for all their staff, what are the specific needs of library staff and which are the generic needs? These questions need to be answered if libraries are to influence and participate in those programmes to maximum effect.

Libraries leading the way

It is very clear that change in academic libraries has been brought about by the same factors which have been at work in universities, colleges and the sector as a whole. Academic libraries have often led the way in responding to these pressures through effective staff development and training. Both Patricia Partington and Robert Oldroyd discuss the early and influential role of librarians in implementing appraisal systems. Patrick Noon recognizes that some libraries have set an example to other departments in providing training programmes for all their staff from their own budgets. Some libraries have led the way in quality initiatives – Aston University Library and Information Service, for example, is acting as a pilot for 'Investors in People' within its institution. The use of the Library Association's CPD framework, described by Julie Parry (see Chapter 2), demonstrates that the potential conflict between individuals, the professional body and the employer can be resolved in the pursuit of continuous improvement which benefits all of them. The possession of professional chartered status should be a powerful quality assurance measure and not an artificial demarcation line.

Systematic management of human resources

This is all very positive. But a number of questions are also raised. In the context of continuous change there is a need for continuous development and training for all staff at every level and at every stage from appointment to retirement. This needs to be based on appropriate appraisal and other systems from which an analysis of needs for all categories of staff can be drawn without breaching the confidentiality of individuals. Comments throughout this book make clear the understanding of the need for such pervasive CPD provision and the recognition that it does not yet exist in all academic libraries. Leading on from this, three key questions emerge.

Systematic management of staff development

First, how systematic is the management of the staff development and training function itself in academic libraries? Is it based on the cyclical management model advocated by Patricia Partington (Chapter 1, *Ways and means*) in which programmes are based on needs analysis and outcomes are evaluated to inform the next cycle?

Integration with human resource management

Secondly, how far is staff development and training integrated with other human resource management functions? Phil Sykes gives an excellent practical example of this when he points out the need to ensure that selection criteria for new staff reflect and do not contradict the skills priorities which appear in our training programmes for existing staff.

Integration with strategic planning

Thirdly, how far is the management of staff development and training integrated with the planning and strategic management processes and systems of academic libraries? As Alison Crook[1] says:

> The one essential point is that all human resources planning should form part of the total organizational planning process. It should be seen by all to flow naturally from the statement of library goals. Identification of needed skills and plans for the development of skills should form an integral part of plans to get the library where it aims to be.

This approach implies that both our annual and project plans and budgets should include specific statements about current and future skill needs and costed proposals for achieving these.

Future issues

The preceding chapters show a remarkable degree of agreement about current issues and resulting training and development needs for the academic library sector. In summary, these major issues emerge:

- customer-focused services;
- developments in new technology;
- teamwork both within and without the library and, in particular, an enhanced role in the teaching/learning delivery team;

- flatter management structures in which accountability both for service delivery and resource management is delegated as far down the 'line' as possible;
- accreditation of work-based learning, for example, through S/NVQs.
- converged services.

Future staff development and training needs

The resulting areas of development and training need may be summarized as follows:

- interpersonal skills focused on dealing effectively both with the external customer and the colleague as customer;
- the ability to exploit new technology fully as information providers and as teachers of information skills;
- leading and working in both function and project-based teams;
- learning theory, course design and delivery methods in order to play a full role in course/module design and delivery;
- management skills of all types;
- upskilling and multiskilling in the context of converged services and of the changing relative roles of qualified staff and support staff;
- training, coaching and assessment skills for staff assuming enhanced roles in work-based learning.

These needs exist for all staff, albeit at different levels and at varying degrees. The list is not exhaustive and the emphasis varies according to the situation of a particular library.

Areas for action

Given this degree of unanimity about issues and needs, how can academic libraries ensure that staff development and training is managed systematically and integrated with other library management processes to address the issues and meet the needs? This, of course, is the 'sixty four thousand dollar question' and the answer perhaps requires a whole book to itself! However, I would like to suggest just five areas for action by academic librarians in partnership with others where appropriate.

Definition of roles

The tasks and responsibilities undertaken by all levels and types of academic library staff have changed enormously over the last decade and are continuing to evolve. Fielden advised that librarians and academics should redefine the boundaries between their relative responsibilities for learner support. This is but one example of the evolution in roles which has been discussed in many of the preceding chapters. This question of role definition becomes all the more crucial in the context of converged services described by Mel Collier (Chapter 6).

There is a need for each service in the light of its strategic plan, to redefine the required roles and responsibilities of each of its staff groups and to do so on a regular basis. In order to be of any use in articulating training needs, this means regularly revised detailed, post and person profiles which specify the tasks and responsibilities of a post (or group of posts) and the skills, knowledge and personal competences required to fulfil them. Together with the information gleaned from appraisal and other systems, this 'manpower' planning model, which has been described fully by Creth and Duda,[2] allows a comparison between skill requirements and the actual skills of existing staff and is a powerful means of training needs analysis. Academic libraries, in common with all university and college departments, now use post profiling, appraisal and CPD systems. The need is for an integrated, coherent approach to their use in order to define skill needs and provide a structured basis for staff recruitment and development planning. In turn, this enables the development of training profiles which describe the generic training needs of groups of staff and define the types of training to be undertaken.

Policies and plans

The second action point is clearly signalled by the Fielden Report. It is the need for libraries to have a staff development policy which gives aims, objectives and priorities for training, defines responsibilities, guaranteed levels of support and policy on whether and which training is mandatory, together with evaluative methods and links to appraisal and review systems. A survey carried out between 1987 and 1988 showed that 62% of the (then) polytechnic libraries had a formal training policy and 33% of the (then) university libraries had one.[3] What is the figure now for the unified sector? But Fielden goes further in asking for human resources to be included more fully in strategic plans. Sheila Corrall,[4] talking about existing plans, comments '. . . many cover staff development and staffing generally, but few present anything resembling a human resources strategy'.

She goes on to note, however, that the problem of poor coverage of human resource issues in strategic plans is not peculiar to universities or their libraries and is a major reason for the introduction of the 'Investors in People' initiative. The influence of the Higher Education Quality Council over universities' planning and quality assurance processes will be an important factor in this area. The plain message is that staff and their development needs should be fully covered in libraries' strategic and operational plans – a move to proactive human resource management.

Resources

Having redefined the roles of staff, analysed the resulting training needs and published policies and plans to meet those needs, what are the resource implications for implementing the resulting ongoing programmes? Fielden makes two recommendations – that a senior member of staff should have formal responsibility for staff development and training and that a minimum of 5% of library staff time should be allocated to training and development.

The need for a senior manager was referred to in the introduction to this book. All too often the responsibility is devolved to someone who operates at the level of 'booking courses' but who is not a member of the library's senior management team, able to link development needs to the overall organizational 'picture' and who has responsibility for other aspects of human resource management such as selection, appraisal and job evaluation. If people are truly as important as budgets and equipment, that is the requirement.

Fielden was perhaps unwise, even with the best of intentions, to specify a mandatory measure for staff development activity. Each library's plan should state the resources required and the rationale for their allocation in order to meet the aims, and objectives on which it is based. A recent Industrial Society survey showed that 40% of organizations (public and private) use days per employee as a measure of training costs, 27% use £s per employee and 20% use percentage of salary bill.[5] Susan Jurow (Chapter 10, *Funding*) shows that few libraries achieve even half of a nationally recommended figure of 2% of total salaries expenditure on training. A 1991–92 survey by the Council of Polytechnic Librarians gave the mean for the same measure as 0.97%.[6] Taking another approach, The Library Association[7] recommends that qualified librarians should have four to six days per year for CPD, of which some is their own time. The crucial point is not the exact level of time or money allocated but that the library has a publicly declared basis for its allocation which results from and is adequate to achieve its strategy. For example, is expenditure on different categories of staff to be strictly equal or will it vary according to factors outlined in an annual training plan?

Commitment

A number of contributors have talked about the uneven staff development and training 'playing-field' which Patricia Partington identified as a key issue in the first chapter. Provision has been uneven, focused on staff categories rather than functions or tasks, and seen as consisting of short courses often provided to cure a problem. She sees the sector as entering a new phase in which coherent CPD programmes, based on functions and roles, are available to all university and college staff throughout their careers. Clearly, that phase is in its early stages. Comments by Julie Parry and Phil Sykes on the paucity of provision to meet the needs of part-time, evening and weekend staff make this point only too clearly. It is only necessary to listen to the arguments about excellence in teaching, definition of teaching competences and whether training in teaching skills should be mandatory, or to follow the debate about accreditation of skills through NVQs, to know that the whole sector is wrestling with the need to reassess and agree functions and tasks and the skills and CPD opportunities required to underpin them. Libraries can use the autonomy which they now have for resource management to lead the way, as they have done in the past, using the systematic approach outlined above. It will not be a comfortable process. Are we willing, for example, to define anew the role of our subject librarians and to specify what teaching and management training will be required at various stages in that career path? Are we willing to make appropriate management training a formal requirement for library managers at all levels?[8] Are we willing to use our budgets to pay for that training and to justify the decision to do so? Will we write the task of CPD for ourselves and others into every one of our post profiles?

Lifelong learning

Libraries have always enabled lifelong learning. My final challenge for academic libraries is to provide the opportunity for lifelong learning for their own staff, to become organizations in which training is not done to people but happens through managers making learning an everyday experience for themselves and their staff.[9] This means the active involvement of all line managers in choice of training events and in ensuring 'training transfer' of skills and knowledge to the job after the event. But it also means that they must provide learning in many different ways on and through the job and, through planned mentoring.

At a national level there is much ad hoc provision through regional training cooperatives, SCONUL, and the Library Association and its groups. There is a lack of coherent, targeted, national programmes such as the models described by Susan Jurow in (Chapter 10, *Education*) and in a recent article by Sheila Corrall.[10] There is a growing need to take up Mel Collier's challenge to provide appropriate programmes for middle and senior managers working in converged services. It is up to us to define what is needed and to work with the Library Association, SCONUL, UCoSDA and others to make sure that it is provided at a national level and to work with our own university staff development managers to shape institutional provision.

Conclusion

Fielden got many of the issues for staff development in academic libraries right, even if he underestimated the sector's awareness of them and the degree to which they are already being addressed. Sadly, the same level of funding for the development of people as is being provided for technology and buildings has not resulted. It is up to academic library managers to determine what happens now by working with and through our institutions' quality procedures, in partnership with other organizations and by managing our staff development with the same strategic skills which we apply to other areas of resource management. We are now in a climate which is receptive, even positively encouraging to the concepts of 'lifelong learning' and 'the learning organization'. As our institutions re-engineer themselves to be providers of lifelong learning for others, so the imperative grows for them to be seen to do the same for their employees.

The essential requirement is for commitment from the institution, the library manager and from individuals to CPD to ensure the personal and organizational renewal which is the most important and effective means of managing change successfully.

References

1   Crook, Alison, 'The development of human resource managers', *Australian academic and research libraries*, **6**, 1985, 86.

2   Creth, Sheila D., and Duda, Frederick, *Personnel administration in libraries*, 2nd edn, New York, Neal-Schuman, 1981, 60.

3   MacDougall, Jennifer, Lewins, Helena and Tseng, Gwyneth, *Continuing education and training opportunities in librarianship*, Boston Spa, Yorkshire, British Library, 1990, 75.

4   Corrall, Sheila, 'Fielden: human resources management', *Library Association record*, **96** (8), 1994, 428–32.

5   'Training data', *Training*, October 1995, 5.

6   Council of Polytechnic Librarians, *Annual statistics 1991–92*, Brighton, COPOL, 1993.

7   Library Association, *Framework for continuing professional development*, London, Library Association, 1992, 28.

8   Wiltenbach, S. A., Bordeianu, S. M. and Wycisk, K., 'Management preparation and training of department head in ARL libraries', *College and research libraries*, **53** (4), Jul. 1992, 319.

9   Taylor, Sally, 'Managing a learning environment', *Personnel management*, **24**, Oct. 1992, 54.

10 Corrall, Sheila, 'Management development in academic libraries', *British journal of academic librarianship*, **9** (3), 1994, 213–6.

Glossary

AALL	American Association of Law Librarians
ACRL	Association of College and Research Libraries
AHUA	Association of Heads of University Administration
ALA	American Library Association
ARL	Association of Research Libraries
ASTD	American Society for Training and Development
AUA	Association of University Administrators
AUT	Association of University Teachers
CCTUT	Coordinating Committee for the Training of University Teachers
CDP	Committee of Directors of Polytechnics
CLR	Council on Library Resources
CMS	Certificate in Management Studies
CNAA	Council for National Academic Awards
CoFHE	Colleges of Further and Higher Education Group
COLT	Council of Library/Media Technicians
COPOL	Council of Polytechnic Librarians
COSHEP	Committee of Scottish Higher Education Principals
CPD	Continuing Professional Development
CVCP	Committee of Vice-Chancellors and Principals
DFEE	Department for Education and Employment
DMS	Diploma in Management Studies
EPSRC	Engineering and Physical Sciences Research Council
ESRC	Economic and Social Research Council
HCLRG	Higher Education Colleges Learning Resources Group
HEI	Higher Education Institution

HEFC	Higher Education Funding Council
HEQC	Higher Education Quality Council
LAMA	Library Administration and Management Association
LITA	Library and Information Technology Association
JANET	Joint Academic Network
JISC	Joint Information Systems Committee
MBA	Masters in Business Administration
MLA	Medical Library Association
MSF	Managerial Scientific and Financial Trade Union
NUPE	National Union of Public Employees
NVQ	National Vocational Qualification
OMS	Office of Management Studies
SCONUL	Standing Conference of National and University Libraries
SEDA	Staff and Educational Development Association
SLA	Special Library Association
SVQ	Scottish Vocational Qualification
SPEC	Systems and Procedures Exchange Center (of the Office of Management Studies)
SRHE	Society for Research in Higher Education
TLTP	Teaching and Learning Technology Programme
TQM	Total Quality Management
UC&R	University College and Research Group
UCISA	Universities and Colleges Information Systems Association
UCNS	Universities Committee for Non-Teaching Staffs
UCoSDA	Universities and Colleges Staff Development Agency
UGC	University Grants Committee

Selective Index